Qualities of an Excellent Servant

Qualities of an Excellent Servant

by
John MacArthur, Jr.

WORD OF GRACE COMMUNICATIONS
P.O. Box 4000
Panorama City, CA 91412

All Scripture quotations, unless noted otherwise, are from the *New Scofield Reference Bible*, King James Version. Copyright © 1967 by Oxford University Press, Inc. Reprinted by permission.

Library of Congress Cataloging in Publication Data

MacArthur, John, 1939-
    Qualities of an excellent servant / by John MacArthur, Jr.
        p.   cm.   — (John MacArthur's Bible studies)
    Bible studies taken from messages delivered by the author at Grace Community Church in Panorama City, Calif.
    Includes indexes.
    ISBN 0-8024-5352-X (pbk.)
    1. Bible. N.T. Timothy, 1st, IV, 1-16—Criticism, interpretation, etc. 2. Clergy—Office—Biblical teaching.
    I. Title. II. Series: MacArthur, John, 1939-   Bible studies.
BS2745.2.M33   1987
227'.8307—dc19   87-25380
                                                                          CIP

1 2 3 4 5 6 7 Printing/LC/Year 91 90 89 88 87

Printed in the United States of America

Contents

These Bible studies are taken from messages delivered by Pastor-Teacher John MacArthur, Jr., at Grace Community Church in Panorama City, California. These messages have been combined into a 6-tape album entitled *Qualities of an Excellent Servant*. You may purchase this series either in an attractive vinyl cassette album or as individual cassettes. To purchase these tapes, request the album *Qualities of an Excellent Servant*, or ask for the tapes by their individual GC numbers. Please consult the current price list; then, send your order, making your check payable to:

WORD OF GRACE COMMUNICATIONS
P.O. Box 4000
Panorama City, CA 91412

Or call the following toll-free number:
1-800-55-GRACE

1

Understanding the Seducing Spirit

Outline

Introduction
A. An Example of Apostasy
B. The Definition of Apostasy
C. The Source of Apostasy
  1. Leviticus 17:7
  2. 1 Corinthians 10:20-21
D. The Confrontation of Apostasy

Lesson
I. The Predictability of Apostates (v. 1*a*)
  A. The Revelation of the Spirit
  B. The Revelation in Scripture
    1. Matthew 24:5
    2. Mark 13:22
    3. 2 Thessalonians 2:3
    4. 2 Peter 3:3
    5. 1 John 2:18-19
II. The Chronology of Apostates (v. 1*b*)
III. The Source of Apostates (v. 1*c*)
  A. The Devotion Described
  B. The Dangers Declared
    1. 2 John 7, 10-11
    2. Jude 23
    3. Deuteronomy 13:12-17
  C. The Demons Discussed
  D. The Doctrines Delineated
IV. The Character of Apostates (v. 2)
  A. Their Hypocrisy (v. 2*a*)
  B. Their Consciences (v. 2*b*)
V. The Teaching of Apostates (v. 3*a*)

Introduction

The first five verses of 1 Timothy 4 are a stern warning about apostates. In verse 6 Paul says to Timothy, "If thou put the brethren in remembrance of these things, thou shalt be a good minister of Jesus Christ." So to be an excellent servant of Christ, it is important that we have a good understanding of apostasy.

A. An Example of Apostasy

Second Chronicles 25 records the account of Amaziah, king of Judah. He was the son of Joash and the father of Uzziah, who was king during the time of Isaiah the prophet. Amaziah reigned in Jerusalem twenty-nine years. Verse 2 says "he did that which was right in the sight of the Lord, but not with a perfect heart." He functioned in accord with the religion of Israel on the outside. He understood it and behaved by its ethics but not with a willing heart. He practiced a heartless, external religion, not having a personal relationship with the living God. So he was soon lured away into idolatry and began to worship the gods of Edom, to which he bowed down and burned incense (v. 14). His life ended tragically—he was murdered by his own people after turning away from the Lord (v. 27).

B. The Definition of Apostasy

Departing from the faith is nothing new. It happens today just as it did in the Old Testament and in the church at Ephesus, where Timothy was when Paul wrote this epistle. There are always people who understand the faith intellectually and behave externally according to the revelation of God but who have no heart for living to please God. Hebrews 3:12 says that those who depart from God demonstrate an unbelieving heart.

Paul states in 1 Timothy 4:1 that some—like Judas, Demas, or the disciples of John 6 who walked no more with Christ—"shall depart from the faith" (Gk., *aphistēmi*, "to remove yourself from the position you originally occupied"). Apostasy isn't an unintentional departure or someone struggling with doubt. It characterizes someone who deliberately abandons truth once affirmed for erroneous teaching. "The faith" refers specifically to the body of Christian doctrine, not the act of believing. Some will depart from "the faith which was once delivered unto the saints" (Jude 3). People who understand and outwardly affirm Christian doctrine but don't have a heart for God are prime candidates for being seduced by demons to depart from the faith.

An apostate is not someone who has never known the truth but someone who has known it and has rejected it. He may have even been involved in various religious activities. But because he has never truly known God, he is lured away by the siren voices of the demons behind idols and false religious systems.

C. The Source of Apostasy

All false religion propagates doctrine energized by seducing spirits. False religion is the playground of demons. Second Corinthians tells us that Satan and his angels disguise themselves as angels of light and become the purveyors of various religions (11:14-15).

1. Leviticus 17:7—The Lord Himself said that whatever people sacrifice to idols is in fact being sacrificed to demons (cf. Deut. 32:17; Ps. 96:5; 106:36-37).

2. 1 Corinthians 10:20-21—Paul said that those who come to the Lord's Table and then worship at a pagan religious shrine are fellowshiping with both the Lord and demons. False religious systems and the various idols that accompany them are simply focal points for demonic activity. You should not naively believe that a false religion is simply a collection of misguided ideas. Realize that fallen angels are energizing false religions behind the scenes, seducing people from the truth into an eternal hell.

The Word of God clearly teaches that apostasy is a demonic seduction, that idol worship is actually worship offered to demons, and that false teachers are the agents of demons. The battle is between God and His truth and the devil and his lies. God calls people to Himself through the truth, and Satan tries to lure people away from truth with his lies.

D. The Confrontation of Apostasy

Scripture often exhorts the church to expose false teaching. That kind of confrontation is not popular today. Many churches in the name of love want to forget disagreements and avoid being critical at all costs. But, nonetheless, there is a biblical mandate to deal with false teaching. The battle lines were drawn in Israel and in the early church, and they must be drawn today too. Like Timothy, we must be warned and instructed to understand what is behind false teaching.

While Timothy was pastoring the church at Ephesus, false teachers were teaching contrary doctrines. From 1 Timothy 1 we learn that they desired to be teachers of the law but didn't understand what they were teaching (v. 7). Verses 18-20 tell us that they had departed from the truth and were delivered to Satan by Paul to learn not to blaspheme. After dealing with false teaching regarding the role of men and women in the church in chapters 2-3, Paul returns to the matter of the false teachers in chapter 4.

First Timothy 3 closes with the theme of truth. Verse 15 states that the church is the pillar and ground of truth, and verse 16 says that Christ is the embodiment of truth. That logically leads into Paul's discussion in chapter 4 of the demonic counterattack against the truth. In the first five verses of chapter 4 he describes the apostates and their teaching, and from verses 6 to 16 he tells Timothy how to be the kind of man necessary to deal with it.

The theme of 1 Timothy 4:1-5 is: "Some shall depart from the faith" (v. 1). Paul warns Timothy to expect apostasy and provides him with six descriptions of apostates so that he can be prepared to identify and counteract them.

Lesson

I. THE PREDICTABILITY OF APOSTATES (v. 1*a*)

"Now the Spirit speaketh expressly."

We should not be shocked to learn that some people will apostatize. The Spirit of God explicitly says that some will depart from the faith. The first word of verse 1, "now" (better translated "but"), heightens the contrast of apostasy to the truths mentioned in the previous verses.

A. The Revelation of the Spirit

The Spirit's explicit instruction in the present tense is a reference to divine revelation. All divine revelation comes from the Holy Spirit. Peter tells us that Scripture is not the product of mankind's ingenuity but of holy men of God guided by the Holy Spirit (2 Pet. 1:21). As Paul penned his epistle to Timothy, the very words of the Holy Spirit about apostasy came through.

Paul knew there would be apostates at the church in Ephesus because the Holy Spirit had revealed that fact to him earlier. Long before he had written this epistle to Timothy, Paul addressed the Ephesian elders with the words: "I know this, that after my departing shall grievous wolves enter in among you, not sparing the flock. Also of your own selves shall men arise, speaking perverse things, to draw away disciples after them" (Acts 20:29-30).

B. The Revelation in Scripture

Such revelation about apostasy was not unique to New Testament times; the Holy Spirit had warned about apostasy back in Old Testament times. Many Scripture verses in the Old Testament talk about Israelites (both individually and nationally) departing from the faith. Although many people belonged to the nation of Israel, that didn't mean they all believed in the God of Israel. Consequently, they were not part of the believing remnant of Israel (cf. Rom. 2:28-29). The Spirit through the centuries of redemptive history has indicated that there would be those who depart from the faith (Deut. 13:12-15; 32:15-18; Dan. 8:23-25).

In the New Testament we find even more references to those who will depart from the faith in the end times.

1. Matthew 24:5—The Lord said, "Many shall come in my name, saying, I am Christ; and shall deceive many."

2. Mark 13:22—In the same context Jesus said, "False Christs and false prophets shall rise, and shall show signs and wonders, to seduce, if it were possible, even the elect."

3. 2 Thessalonians 2:3—Paul informed us that before the coming of Christ in glory there will be a massive departure from the faith.

4. 2 Peter 3:3—Peter said there will come in the last times scoffers, abandoning the faith to pursue their own lusts (cf. Jude 18).

5. 1 John 2:18-19—John said forerunners of the Antichrist will depart from the faith, revealing that they were not truly Christians to begin with.

It is inevitable that people will make a momentary response to biblical truth, like the seed that went into the rocky ground (Matt. 13:20-21). But because they have no root, no living union with God, they die out. And there are others whose spiritual pursuits are choked out by the cares of this world and the love of riches. Such kinds of people may hang around a while, but since their hearts are not given to God they are seduced away by demonic spirits through the human agency of false teachers.

II. THE CHRONOLOGY OF APOSTATES (v. 1b)

"In the latter times."

That phrase does not refer to a long time in the future but to the church age, the time between the first and second comings of Christ. The apostle John said, "Little children, it is the last time" (1 John 2:18). Peter said Christ "was manifest in these last times for you" (1 Pet. 1:20). Hebrews 1:2 declares that God has "in these last days spoken unto us by his Son." Hebrews also states that "in the end of the ages [Christ] appeared to put away sin by the sacrifice of himself" (Heb. 9:26).

All those verses tell us that the last times began when Christ first appeared and initiated the messianic era. He is now building His kingdom in the hearts of believers and will return to establish it on the earth and then in the eternal state. So we are now living in the last times. It is in this dispensation or age that the apostasy to which Paul is referring will occur.

III. THE SOURCE OF APOSTATES (v. 1c)

"Giving heed to seducing spirits, and doctrines of demons."

Apostates listen to seducing spirits and the teachings of demons. The source of apostasy is demonic. Paul described the supernatural battle with demonic forces when he said, "We wrestle not against flesh and blood, but against principalities, against powers, against the rulers of the darkness of this world, against spiritual wickedness in high places" (Eph. 6:12).

People with "an evil heart of unbelief [depart] from the living God" (Heb. 3:12) because they are lured away by demon spirits, even though there is a facade of religion. Such people cannot be wooed by the Spirit of God because of their hard-hearted unbelief and fall prey to Satan and his lies transmitted through his demons.

A. The Devotion Described

The term "giving heed" doesn't merely mean "to give attention to"; it means "to give assent to." It conveys the idea of devoting or attaching oneself to a person or thing. Its use in the present tense implies a continual clinging to the seductive doctrines that the spirits disseminate.

An apostate in the context of the New Testament is a person who understands the gospel and who may outwardly identify with the Christian faith. But because his heart is not truly God's, he turns from the truth to the lies of the devil and is drawn away from the true faith unto eternal damnation.

The Devil Made Him Do It

I often hear parents say, "Our child was raised in a Christian home, but when he went away to college he was led astray by atheistic professors (or religious cult leaders) and now denies the faith." Such students aren't the victims of erudite and persuasive professors, religious leaders, or clever writers who have subtly propagated falsehoods in textbooks. Ungodly philosophies and false religions are not merely human aberrations; they are ultimately the product of Satan himself.

B. The Dangers Declared

We should be immensely cautious about exposing ourselves or anyone we love to false teaching. Many Scripture verses warn us of the dangers of false teachers.

1. 2 John 7, 10-11—The apostle John gave us a warning about false teachers and how we should respond to them: "Many deceivers are entered into the world, who confess not that Jesus Christ cometh in the flesh. . . . If there come any unto you, and bring not this doctrine, receive him not into your house, neither bid him Godspeed; for he that biddeth him Godspeed is partaker of his evil deeds." Stay away from false teachers.

2. Jude 23—Anytime you are near people who are under the influence of false teachers, you should yank them out of the fire, so to speak, exercising caution that you yourself don't get burned in the process.

3. Deuteronomy 13:12-17—The Lord warned the nation of Israel about false prophets through Moses, saying, "If thou shalt hear a report in one of thy cities, which the Lord thy God hath given thee to dwell there, saying, Certain men, worthless fellows, are gone out from among you, and have withdrawn the inhabitants of their city, saying, Let us go and serve other gods, which ye have not known, then shalt thou inquire, and make

search, and ask diligently; and, behold, if it be truth, and the thing certain, that such abomination is wrought among you, thou shalt surely smite the inhabitants of that city with the edge of the sword, destroying it utterly, and all that is therein, and the cattle thereof, with the edge of the sword. And thou shalt gather all the spoil of it into the midst of the street thereof, and shalt burn with fire the city, and all the spoil thereof every whit, for the Lord thy God, and it shall be an heap forever; it shall not be built again. And there shall cling nothing of the cursed thing to thine hand; that the Lord may turn from the fierceness of his anger, and show upon thee mercy, and have compassion upon thee." You know God is serious about false doctrine, since He instructed the Israelites to go to the extreme of burning the city after slaying its inhabitants and cattle so that it could never be rebuilt.

C. The Demons Discussed

The phrase "seducing spirits" refers to the source of false doctrines—supernatural demonic spirit beings who are fallen angels. "Seducing" is a translation of the Greek term from which we get our word *planet*. It conveys the idea of wandering and is applied to those spirits who would lead you to wander from the truth by seducing or deceiving you. Whereas the Holy Spirit guides us into truth (John 16:13), these spirits lead people into error. They are the principalities and powers that the church must wrestle against (Eph. 6:11-12).

The history of seducing spirits goes all the way back to the Garden of Eden, where Satan seduced Eve into believing she was being cheated out of the best thing God had by not being able to eat from the forbidden tree (Gen. 3:1-6). He seduced her into disobeying God's instruction to her. Such seductions are chronicled throughout Scripture, all the way to the book of Revelation.

D. The Doctrines Delineated

False teachers seduce people with the "doctrines of demons." The world is full of demonic teaching. Anything that contradicts the Word of God is ultimately a teaching from demons. They're behind it all. False teaching doesn't come from clever people. It comes from demons. That's why exposing yourself to it is more dangerous than you might believe.

However, not all demonic teaching looks demonic on the surface. Some of it is so subtly disguised that we might not even recognize it as such unless we look closely. Many people are trifling with satanic doctrines without knowing it and will be seduced unless such false teaching is exposed.

IV. THE CHARACTER OF APOSTATES (v. 2)

A. Their Hypocrisy (v. 2a)

"Speaking lies in hypocrisy."

The doctrines of demons are dispensed through human agents. Although the source is supernatural, the means of seduction is natural—occurring on the human level. The beginning phrase of verse 2 can best be translated "through the hypocrisy of men that speak lies." Demons use men and women who may appear to be well educated or religious. These individuals may be preachers or priests who are moral and devout in appearance. They may give the impression that their motives are pure in their desire to help people. But the facade of religiosity serves only to hide the demonic error behind that mask. Hypocritical teachers may seem to be exalting God, but it is actually Satan whom they exalt. They are deceivers and liars who come masked in religious garb, possibly even teaching at a Christian church or school, or writing a book aimed toward a Christian audience. They will find an audience and propagate their hellish doctrines under the direction of seducing spirits.

B. Their Consciences (v. 2b)

"Having their conscience seared with a hot iron."

Some commentators believe that phrase alludes to the ancient practice of branding slaves on their foreheads and therefore implies that such hypocrites are the devil's agents.

Although that meaning makes sense, I believe it is better to understand the phrase as referring to more than just ownership by Satan. The conscience is the part of a person that affirms or condemns an action and thus controls behavior. False teachers can carry on their hypocrisy day after day because their consciences have been scarred beyond the ability to discern right and wrong. They have lost their sensitivity to truth and integrity.

The Greek word for "seared" (*kausteriazō*) is the medical term Hippocrates used for the cauterizing process—the searing of body tissue or blood vessels with heat. False teachers have been scarred to the point that they can carry on their hypocritical lies with no compunction.

In my own ministry I am concerned about my responsibility to speak the truth of God. I regularly pray that every time I teach God's Word I would not utter anything that is untrue. My conscience demands that I deal with truth carefully because it's God's truth, and people's souls are at stake. Yet there are some who never investigate the accuracy of what they teach because their consciences have been desensitized to the truth by having been constantly abused. Their apostasy has scarred their consciences.

V. THE TEACHING OF APOSTATES (v. 3*a*)

"Forbidding to marry, and commanding to abstain from foods."

Those restrictions are just a sample of their erroneous doctrines. Some false teachers taught that if you wanted to be spiritual you shouldn't marry and you should abstain from certain kinds of food. It is typical of Satan to take something that may be appropriate for certain people at certain times and make it mandatory for everyone. Paul honors singleness in 1 Corinthians 7, and Jesus acknowledges the place for fasting with the proper motives in Matthew 6. But the apostates Paul mentions in 1 Timothy 4 were requiring ascetic self-denial to attain spirituality. Salvation for them was based on what they denied themselves.

All false religions devise human means by which you become saved, either by things you do or don't do. They are all ultimately based on human achievement. Although ascetic practices may give the impression of spiritual sincerity, they aren't the means of attaining holiness.

As early as 166 B.C. the Essene sect of Judaism was living in an isolated community by the Dead Sea. It emphasized an ascetic life-style of marital and dietary abstinence. Such thinking may have found its way to Ephesus. However the church was probably most directly influenced by Greek Gnosticism, which held that spirit is good and matter is evil. So those who adhered to that philosophy denied themselves physical pleasures such as marital relations and certain foods. They believed such abstinence would please their deities. That erroneous philosophy was probably what influenced the Corinthians on the topics of marriage (1 Cor. 7) and bodily resurrection (1 Cor. 15).

Such externalism is typical of false religion. Paul's point at the end of verse 3 is that spirituality is not related to what you accept or deny yourself in terms of things given by God for your enjoyment. In Colossians 2:16-23 he says, "Let no man, therefore, judge you in food, or in drink, or in respect of a feast day, or of the new moon, or of a sabbath day, which are a shadow of things to come; but the body [reality] is of Christ. Let no man beguile you of your reward in a voluntary humility and worshiping of angels . . . [or subject you] to ordinances (touch not; taste not; handle not; which all are to perish with the using) after the commandments and doctrines of men." Don't follow the ascetic approach of trying to earning your acceptance before God. As a Christian you are already complete in Christ (Col. 2:10). True religion acknowledges that the Lord alone has accomplished our salvation. False religion says we've got to do it ourselves by self-denial and human achievement.

VI. THE ERROR OF APOSTATES (vv. 3*b*-5)

A. Failing to Understand the Purpose of God's Creation (v. 3*b*)

"God hath created [marriage and foods] to be received with thanksgiving by them who believe and know the truth."

God created marriage when He provided a wife for Adam. Both Paul and Peter stressed the importance of a good marriage relationship (1 Cor. 7:1-5; Eph. 5:22-33; 1 Pet. 3:7). God provided a variety of foods for mankind's nourishment and enjoyment (Gen. 1:29; 9:3). In fact, when God created the earth, He declared that the products of His handiwork were "very good" (Gen. 1:31). It doesn't make sense to deny mankind what God has created to be received with thanksgiving.

Although God designed the blessings of marriage and food for all people, only those who believe and know the truth give God thanks for what He has provided. God designed marriage and a wide variety of foods so He would be glorified. The world eats the food and enjoys marriage without considering the One who gave those good gifts. Only those who are thankful to God bring Him glory, so in the truest sense marriage, food, and every other good thing God made were designed specially for believers. The world does benefit from God's blessings—He sends rain on the just and the unjust (Matt. 5:45)—but its unbelieving inhabitants were never the ultimate reason God gave good things.

It is ludicrous to deny the right to marriage and certain foods in an attempt to attain holiness because that's to deny God the right to be glorified for the beauty of what He gave us. It would be better to be married and eat everything He provided and praise Him for them than believe you're holy by abstaining from those things.

B. Failing to Understand the Nature of God's Creation (vv. 4-5)

1. Its excellence (v. 4)

"Every creature of God is good, and nothing is to be refused, if it is received with thanksgiving."

The Greek word translated "good" (*kalos*) means "inherently excellent." Marriage and food are inherently good and should not be rejected but gratefully accepted.

2. Its sanctification (v. 5)

"It is sanctified by the word of God and prayer."

"The word of God" is used in the pastoral epistles to refer to the gospel of Jesus Christ. The message of salvation clarifies that all the dietary laws have been abolished. They were given for a brief time in Israel's history to develop their moral faculty of discernment and to make them distinct from other nations. But once Christ came and fulfilled the sacrificial laws and made Jew and Gentile one in Him, those dietary laws were set aside. They had a limited national purpose. To reimpose them is to manufacture a works-righteousness system and dishonor God by saying He created something evil.

If we understand that the gospel has freed us from dietary laws and if in prayer we offer God thanks, then we can receive any and all of His good gifts. Mandatory celibacy and abstinence from certain foods is demonic teaching—denies the goodness of God's creation and His desire for thanks and praise.

External self-denial is a severe error that is typical of false religions. The error of apostates is in believing that they please God by following and teaching such pharisaical practices. Instead they are actually displeasing God and following the lies of demons. Although King Amaziah of Judah did the right things on the outside, he never had a heart for God. He turned away from the Lord. We need to evaluate the condition of our own hearts to make sure we aren't committing the same error he did.

Focusing on the Facts

1. What kind of religion did Amaziah practice (see p. 8)?
2. What is an apostate (see p. 9)?
3. What spiritual entities do people actually worship in false religions? Support your answer with Scripture (see p. 9).
4. What phrase constitutes the theme of 1 Timothy 4:1-5 (v. 1; see p. 10)?
5. Why should we not be surprised to learn that some people will apostatize (see p. 11)?
6. What had Paul written earlier about the effect of apostasy on the church at Ephesus (see p. 11)?
7. Did all Israelites believe in God? Explain, supporting your answer with Scripture (see pp. 11-12).

8. Cite some Scripture verses that give evidence of the abundance of false religions and apostates in the end times (see p. 12).
9. To what period of time does the phrase "latter times" refer (1 Tim. 4:1; see pp. 12-13)?
10. What is the source of false teaching (see p. 13)?
11. What kind of people fall prey to Satan and his lies (Heb. 3:12; see p. 13)?
12. How do 2 John, Jude, and Deuteronomy convey the serious dangers of apostasy (see pp. 14-15)?
13. Whereas the Holy Spirit guides us into _____ (John 16:3), seducing spirits lead people into _____ (see p. 15).
14. Why is exposing yourself to false teaching so dangerous (see p. 16)?
15. How are demonic doctrines dispensed? How have their consciences been seared (1 Tim. 4:2; see pp. 16-17)?
16. What are some of the restrictions false teachers had placed upon their followers (1 Tim. 4:3a; see p. 17)?
17. What means of salvation do false religions devise (see p. 17)?
18. Identify and explain the philosophy that probably influenced the false religion at Ephesus (see p. 18).
19. What did the false teachers fail to understand about the purpose of God's creation (see p. 19)?
20. What two things did the false teachers fail to understand about the nature of God's creation? Explain each (see pp. 19-20).

Pondering the Principles

1. How do you respond to false teaching? Are you more concerned about avoiding controversy than exposing demonic systems that lead naive souls to eternal damnation? When Jesus encountered religious leaders who were misleading and taking advantage of the unsuspecting, His zeal for the truth led him to confront them with their hypocrisy (Matt. 23; John 2:13-17). When you seek to speak of Christ to those who have been led astray and snatch them before they fall into the fires of hell, have a healthy fear of the destructiveness and deceptiveness of their erroneous beliefs (Jude 23). Like the fire fighter who is injured while putting out the fire, we must take care that the false teaching we are combating does not engulf us by causing us to doubt the truth and stop effectively serving the Lord.

2. What have you been trusting to secure your place in heaven? Is it self-denial or the good deeds you have done? Is Christianity simply a matter of the things you don't do? Have you been deceived into believing you must do good works to gain and maintain your salvation? The gospel of Jesus Christ offers salvation to all by grace through faith in Him alone (Eph. 2:8-9). Search your heart for the motive that you associate with Christians. Is it to know, love, and serve God better? If you are a Christian, make sure you are thanking Him for your freedom to enjoy the good gifts He has provided. What things in your life that you previously had taken for granted took on new meaning when you became a Christian? Offer Him thanks and praise for them today.

2

Qualities of an Excellent Servant—Part 1

Outline

Introduction
A. Excellent Service
B. Willing Service
C. Positive Service

Lesson
I. The Excellent Servant Warns People of Error (v. 6*a*)
   A. The Act of Reminding
      1. The resource identified
      2. The resource ignored
   B. The Accountability of Reminding
II. The Excellent Servant Is an Expert Student of Scripture (v. 6*b*)
   A. The Past Examined
   B. The Process Explained
      1. 1 Peter 2:2
      2. 2 Timothy 2:15
      3. Ephesians 6:17
      4. Colossians 3:16
      5. 2 Timothy 3:16-17
   C. The Preparation Evaluated
   D. The Pursuit Exemplified
III. The Excellent Servant Avoids the Influence of Unholy Teaching (v. 7*a*)
   A. A Contradiction of the Truth
   B. A Commitment to the Truth
IV. The Excellent Servant Disciplines Himself in Personal Godliness (vv. 7*b*-9)
   A. The Exhortation (v. 7*b*)
      1. "Exercise"
         a) Training for esteem

Introduction

In 1 Timothy 4:6-16 the apostle Paul lists the qualifications of an excellent servant of Jesus Christ. The key phrase appears in verse 6: "Thou shalt be a good minister of Jesus Christ." In a sense, it's the underlying theme of the whole epistle, which was written to instruct Timothy on how to minister to the church at Ephesus.

A. Excellent Service

The Greek word translated "good" could better be translated "noble," "admirable," or "excellent." It is used back in 1 Timothy 3:1 to speak of the work of ministry and to identify the kind of man to be in ministry.

"Minister" is the translation of the Greek word *diakonos*, from which we get the English word *deacon*. It means "servant" and is used of those who hold the office of deacon in the church, as described in chapter 3. Although the word is not used here in a technical way to designate that office, it implies that anyone who serves in any capacity in ministry must see himself as a servant of the Lord Jesus Christ.

B. Willing Service

The word *diakonos* is different from the word *doulos*, which is also often translated "servant." Whereas *doulos* often refers to a slave under subjection, *diakonos* emphasizes a servant with a higher degree of freedom who serves willingly. The word conveys the idea of usefulness and implies that all Christians willingly pursue usefulness to the cause of Jesus Christ. In 1 Corinthians 4:1-2 Paul says, "Let a man so account of us, as of the ministers of Christ, and stewards of the mysteries of God. Moreover, it is required in stewards, that a man be found faithful." We are called to be servants and stewards, managing that which belongs to God in a way that will bring honor to His name. Paul's instruction to Timothy is applicable for all who serve the Lord.

C. Positive Service

In 1 Timothy 4:1-5 Paul talks about doctrines of demons propagated by seducing spirits through lying hypocrites. Having warned Timothy that false teaching isn't human but demonic, he then tells Timothy how to be a good and effective minister in the face of false doctrine. Yet in instructing Timothy on how to deal with false doctrine, he majors on the positive, not on the negative. Rather than encouraging Timothy to develop a defensive ministry of refuting and denouncing error, Paul emphasizes taking the offensive approach by teaching the Word of God (vv. 6, 11, 13, 16). That tells me that ministry must primarily involve building up the people of God—not exclusively identifying and attacking error. That can be difficult, especially if you are committed to the truth. I have to constantly resist the temptation to denounce the many things that bother me and focus on establishing the truth in the hearts and minds of those I teach. I believe teaching the truth provides the basis for being able to spot error. The emphasis of ministry is to be positive.

In verses 6-16 Paul gives eleven characteristics of being an excellent minister of Christ. They are practical and helpful objectives for everyone who desires to serve the Lord by leading His people.

Lesson

I. THE EXCELLENT SERVANT WARNS PEOPLE OF ERROR (v. 6a)

"If thou put the brethren in remembrance of these things."

A. The Act of Reminding

Although the ministry is not to be dominated by a negative approach, that doesn't mean there isn't a place for warning others about the destructiveness of false doctrine. Paul makes a transition from exposing demonic doctrines to explaining how to be an excellent servant of Jesus Christ by instructing Timothy to warn the church about such doctrines. There is a necessity to remind Christians of error. Ministry demands warning.

The Greek word translated "to put in remembrance of" means "to lay before." Its use here as a present participle speaks of continually reminding people of the reality of false doctrine. There is no idea of commanding people but of giving them counsel and advice in a gentle, humble manner. A servant of Christ must teach people to be discerning by encouraging them to think biblically and to discern between truth and error.

1. The resource identified

Identifying error is not to be the theme of the average pastor's ministry but a recurring reminder. When Paul met with the Ephesian elders he said, "I know this, that after my departing shall grievous wolves enter in among you, not sparing the flock. Also of your own selves shall men arise, speaking perverse things, to draw away disciples after them. Therefore, watch, and remember, that for the space of three years I ceased not to warn everyone night and day with tears. And now, brethren, I commend you to God, and to the word of his grace, which is able to build you up" (Acts 20:29-32). Paul continually made the Ephesians aware of error and pointed them to the positive solution of the Word. The truth supplies the foundation from which error can be dealt with properly.

Christians are prevented from being "children, tossed to and fro, and carried about with every wind of doctrine" (Eph. 4:14) by being firmly grounded in the Word of God. First John 2:13-14 reinforces the fact that a believer learns to deal with satanic error by being strong in the Word, which is the sword of the Spirit. That's the only way to fight and win against beings who disguise themselves as angels of light and ministers of righteousness (2 Cor. 11:14-15).

2. The resource ignored

I believe the church's failure to be discerning in this generation has allowed it to be infiltrated by all kinds of error. It is confused, weak, and in some cases apostate. In many churches you hear watered-down sermons. Limp theology and preaching that lacks conviction have replaced strong doctrine and clear exposition of Scripture. The legacy has been tragic. The church has been flooded with charismatic confusion, unbiblical psychology, cultic influences, success-oriented philosophy, prosperity doctrines, and man-centered theology.

B. The Accountability of Reminding

The church must draw the lines between error and truth and build up its people in the Word of God. God holds pastors accountable to warn their people of spiritual danger. The Lord told Ezekiel, "Son of man, I have made thee a watchman unto the house of Israel; therefore, hear the word at my mouth and give them warning from me. When I say to the wicked, Thou shalt surely die; and thou givest him not warning, nor speakest to warn the wicked from his wicked way, to save his life, the same wicked man shall die in his iniquity, but his blood will I require at thine hand" (Ezek. 3:17-18). If spiritual leaders fail to do that, they will have to answer to God (Heb. 13:17). Although the church today seems to embrace everything—including error—the man of God must develop convictions based upon a biblical theology and continually warn his people of error. He is committed to protecting the flock.

II. THE EXCELLENT SERVANT IS AN EXPERT STUDENT OF SCRIPTURE (v. 6b)

"Nourished up in the words of faith and of good doctrine, unto which thou hast attained."

A. The Past Examined

An excellent minister is also an expert student of Scripture. It's hard for me to understand how the church lost touch with that fact. Sad to say, many Christian pastors have a minimal understanding of Scripture and little commitment to studying it. There was a day in the history of the church when the great students of Scripture and theology were pastors. In the Puritan era pastors were producing many excellent books on doctrine and theology. Rather than being just good communicators, they were first and foremost students of God's Word. They had the capability of understanding, interpreting, and applying the Word of God with great precision and wisdom.

B. The Process Explained

The Greek word translated "nourished up" is a present passive participle, implying that being nourished with the Word of God is a continual process of feeding. That involves reading Scripture, meditating on it, dialoguing over it, and studying it until you've mastered its contents.

It is essential that we be continually nourished by "the words of faith." That phrase refers to the body of Christian truth in Scripture. We are to master Scripture. We'll never do it, but that's our pursuit. We are to be experts in that area, not just good communicators who can tickle people's ears and make them believe they heard something enjoyable (2 Tim. 4:3). We need to accurately interpret and defend the Word of God. Not only are we to be nourished directly by "the words of faith" but also by "good doctrine" (Gk., *kalē didaskalia*). "Good doctrine" encompasses the teaching of biblical truth and the application of its principles. Spiritual growth is based upon our interaction with biblical truth.

1. 1 Peter 2:2—We grow spiritually as we study the Bible.

2. 2 Timothy 2:15—Paul said, "Study to show thyself approved unto God, a workman that needeth not to be ashamed, rightly dividing the word of truth." We are

called—above and beyond all other elements in the ministry—to be expert students of the Word of God.

3. Ephesians 6:17—We are to bear "the sword of the Spirit, which is the word of God" and be able to use it in any way at any time.

4. Colossians 3:16—We are to have the Word of Christ dwelling in us richly and deeply.

5. 2 Timothy 3:16-17—Since the Word of God "is profitable for doctrine, for reproof, for correction, for instruction in righteousness, that the man of God may be perfect, thoroughly furnished unto all good works," then we must know it.

To be able to think and speak biblically a pastor has to spend a large proportion of his time interacting with Scripture. It is an inexhaustible treasure that demands a lifetime just to begin to understand its full riches. There is no virtue in being ignorant. Unfortunately we are a generation of people who do not like to sit and think; we prefer to be entertained. In spite of that, we are to be committed to studying, understanding, and articulating the Word of God.

C. The Preparation Evaluated

The phrase "unto which thou hast attained" in verse 6 is better translated "which you have been following" (NASB*). Paul acknowledged that Timothy was already on schedule. Timothy had originally been taught spiritual truths from his mother and grandmother when he was a boy (2 Tim. 1:5; 3:14-15). Paul himself had been instrumental in teaching Timothy (2 Tim. 2:2). He encouraged him to continue being nourished by that same Christian truth revealed in God's Word.

The excellent pastor continually feeds on divine truth. He cannot give out what he does not take in. The better learner he is, the better teacher he will be. A Bible teacher must spend many more hours in preparation than he actually spends in teaching. That is the natural application of

*New American Standard Bible.

29

Jesus' command to make disciples, teaching them to observe everything He had commanded them (Matt. 28:20).

Sadly, there are many men who have no delight in their studies. They spend an hour studying now and then or no time at all. Study seems for many an unwelcome task that interrupts the easy schedule of activity. They like to have guests as often as possible in their pulpits so they don't have to spend time studying and prefer the variety of administrative tasks and meetings. And the minimal study that they do produces weak sermons that fail to penetrate the hearts and minds of listeners.

D. The Pursuit Exemplified

Since the Bereans were considered noble because they searched the Scriptures daily (Acts. 17:10-11), how much more should those who are in the role of teachers study them! The great men of God who have left their imprint on the church through the years have been those who have had a great understanding of Scripture. William Tyndale, the man responsible for getting the New Testament translated into the English language in 1525, was in prison facing martyrdom. He wrote a letter to the governor in chief, asking that these possessions be sent to him: a warmer cap, a warmer coat, and a piece of cloth to patch his leggings. Then he said, "But most of all I beg and beseech and entreat your clemency to be urgent with the commissary, that he will kindly permit me to have the Hebrew bible, Hebrew grammar, and Hebrew dictionary, that I may pass the time in that study" (J. F. Mozley, *William Tyndale* [New York: Macmillan, 1937], p. 334). Any seminary student who has struggled with Hebrew cannot relate to such a request! But later in life when you plunge more deeply into the Word of God, it's wonderful to be able to say that what you cherish most is what helps you understand the Word of God the best. That was the desire of Paul as he encouraged Timothy.

III. THE EXCELLENT SERVANT AVOIDS THE INFLUENCE OF UNHOLY TEACHING (v. 7*a*)

"Refuse profane and old wives' fables."

A. A Contradiction of the Truth

As strong as a servant of God is in the Word, he is inversely disinterested in unholy teaching. The Greek word translated "profane" (*bebēlos*) refers to something radically separate from what is holy, particularly anything that contradicts the Word of God. "Fables" is a translation of the Greek word *muthos*, from which the English word *myth* is derived. Second Timothy 4:4 says that some "shall turn away their ears from the truth, and shall be turned unto fables." So truth and fables are seen as opposites. The Christian is to be nourished by the truth and refuse that which opposes it.

The identification of fables with old women has a cultural meaning. The phrase was used in philosophical circles as a sarcastic epithet when one wanted to heap disdain on a particular viewpoint. It conveyed the picture of a senile old woman telling a fairy tale to a child and therefore was applied to things lacking credibility.

B. A Commitment to the Truth

The mind is a precious thing. God wants those who serve as spiritual leaders to have pure minds saturated with the truth of His Word. There's no place for foolish myths or unholy contradictions to the truth. Yet somehow our society would rather follow them than biblical truth.

Too Much Bible?

The mark of theological scholarship in some circles is no longer how well a man knows the Bible but how well he understands the speculations of the secular academic establishment.

When I was considering completing a doctoral degree in theology, the representative of the graduate program at the college looked over my transcripts and concluded I had had too much Bible and theology in my undergraduate work. So he gave me a list of two hundred books of preparatory reading before I could be admitted to the program. I checked out the list with someone who knew the various titles and learned that none of them contained anything but liberal theology and humanistic philosophy—they were full of profane old wives' fables passed off as scholarship! The college also required me to take a course called "Jesus and the Cinema." That involved watching contemporary movies and evaluating them on whether they were antagonistic to or supportive of the Jesus ethic. The divine Jesus had been reduced to an ethic! I met with the representative again and said, "I just want to let you know that I have spent all my life to this point learning the truth, and I can't see any value in spending the next couple of years learning error."

I'm grateful to God that from the beginning of my training right on through to today, my mind has been filled with the truth of God. My mind is not a battleground of indecision about what is true and what is false, over things "which minister questions rather than godly edifying" (1 Tim. 1:4). I can speak with conviction because there's no equivocation in my mind. I have avoided the plethora of supposed intellectuals and scholars who disagree with biblical truth. However, one man I knew had problems in that area. He went to a liberal seminary to prepare for ministry but came out a bartender. The confusion of liberalism had destroyed his motivation to serve God. Your mind is a precious thing, and it needs to be kept clear from satanic lies. The excellent minister maintains his biblical convictions and clarity of mind by exposing himself to the Word of God.

IV. THE EXCELLENT SERVANT DISCIPLINES HIMSELF IN PERSONAL GODLINESS (vv. 7b-9)

A. The Exhortation (v. 7b)

"Exercise thyself rather unto godliness."

J. Oswald Sanders says in his book *Spiritual Leadership*, "Spiritual ends can be achieved only by spiritual men who employ spiritual methods" ([Chicago: Moody, 1980], p. 40). The issue in ministry is godliness. It isn't how clever you are or how well you communicate; it's whether you know the Word of God and are leading a godly life. Ministry is an overflow of the latter.

1. "Exercise"

   a) Training for esteem

   The English word *gymnasium* comes from the Greek word translated "exercise" (*gumnazō*), used of those who trained themselves in athletic endeavors. It implies a rigorous, self-sacrificing kind of training. In Greek culture, the gymnasium was a focal point of the city for youths between the ages of sixteen and eighteen. Since athletic ability was highly esteemed, there was usually a gymnasium in every town. The cultic exaltation of the body resulted in a preoccupation with exercise and athletic training and competition, not dissimilar to our own day.

   b) Training for godliness

   Paul alluded to that cultural reality in exhorting Timothy to exercise himself for the goal of godliness, saying in effect, "If you're going to go into training, concentrate on training your inner nature for godliness." The Greek work for godliness is *eusebeia* and means "reverence," "piety," or "true spiritual virtue." "Keep yourself in training for godliness" would be an accurate way to translate Paul's exhortation to Timothy.

   (1) 1 Corinthians 9:27—Paul understood the importance of discipline in the ministry: "I buffet my body and make it my slave, lest possibly, after I have preached to others, I myself should be disqualified" (NASB). How many men in the ministry have that goal? There's no great longing for holiness or a willingness to pursue it. So many ministers are more preoccupied with the externals and lack the necessary spiritual discipline.

   (2) 2 Corinthians 7:1—Paul exhorted all Christians to be "perfecting holiness in the fear of God." That requires building up the spiritual nature to be strong and capable in doing the will of God.

33

(3) 2 Timothy 2:3-5—Paul told Timothy to "endure hardness as a good soldier of Jesus Christ. No man that warreth entangleth himself with the affairs of this life, that he may please him who hath chosen him to be a soldier. And if a man also strive for masteries, yet is he not crowned, except he strive lawfully." As a soldier endures hardship, makes sacrifices, and cuts himself off from the world to please the one who enlisted him; and as an athlete must diligently train and compete within the rules, so must a servant of God make sacrifices in disciplining himself and confining himself to God's standards.

2. "Godliness"

(This point is discussed in chap. 3.)

B. The Explanation (v. 8)

1. The minimal benefit of physical exercise (v. 8a)

"Bodily exercise profiteth little."

Physical exercise profits little in two ways: extent and duration. In extent, it benefits only the body and not the spirit. In duration, it's good only for a short time. You could spend years getting yourself in shape, but as soon as you let up, you immediately start losing what you've worked so hard to achieve.

2. The maximum benefit of spiritual exercise (v. 8b)

"But godliness is profitable unto all things, having promise of the life that now is, and of that which is to come."

Godliness is profitable not only for the body but for the soul as well. It's profitable not just for a brief time but for this lifetime and the rest of eternity. If you're going to make a New Year's resolution, don't resolve to go to the gym three times a week if you're not spending time in the Word of God every day and cultivating godliness. The present benefit of spiritual discipline is a fulfilled,

God-blessed, fruitful, and useful life. If you get involved in spiritual gymnastics, the blessings of godliness will carry on into eternity. Although many people spend far more time exercising their bodies than their souls, the excellent servant of Jesus Christ realizes that spiritual discipline is a priority.

C. The Evaluation (v. 9)

"This is a faithful saying and worthy of all acceptance."

That's a formula Paul used four other times in the pastoral epistles (1 Tim. 1:15; 3:1; 2 Tim. 2:11; Titus 3:8). "Worthy of all acceptance" adds emphasis to his affirmation. It identifies a trustworthy statement or an axiom that is patently obvious. This formula was used to introduce proverbial statements that were commonly understood and used in the church. One example is seen in 1 Timothy 3:1: "This is a true saying, If a man desire the office of a bishop [elder], he desireth a good work."

The greater benefit of spiritual discipline is an obvious truth. The introductory formula of verse 9 refers back to verse 8, rather than to verse 10. Verse 8 is more proverbial in style, using common words in a simple format that would be easy to memorize. Also the phrase "for, therefore" at the beginning of verse 10, along with a statement of personal labor and struggle, makes it less suitable as a "faithful saying" than verse 8.

It is spiritually immature to preoccupy ourselves with our bodies. Doing so betrays a limited perception of spiritual and eternal realities. It should be axiomatic in the church that Christians are a group of people who are in spiritual training to be conformed to the will of God, not a group of body worshipers.

Godliness is the pursuit of the excellent minister. He uses all the means of grace available—prayer, Bible study, the Lord's Table, confession of sin, active service, accountability, and sometimes fasting—in the discipline of godliness.

What then makes an excellent minister? Is it the size of his church? Is it whether he's on radio and television or whether he's a dynamic speaker? God's evaluation is: Is he discerning and does he warn his people about error? Is he diligent in studying Scripture? Does he have a pure mind and avoid the influence of unholy teaching? And does he rigorously exercise himself to be godly? That's the stuff of which an excellent minister is made.

Focusing on the Facts

1. What is an underlying theme of 1 Timothy (see p. 24)?
2. In instructing Timothy on how to deal with false doctrine, Paul majors on a positive approach to ministry. What can we learn from that (see p. 25)?
3. A servant of Christ must encourage people to think biblically and be able to discern between _____ and _____ (see p. 26).
4. Although Paul made certain to warn the Ephesians about false teachers, to what positive solution did he point them (Acts 20:29-32; see p. 26)?
5. Who is held accountable for warning a church of doctrinal errors (see p. 27)?
6. How do many pastors today differ from Puritan pastors in their general commitment to studying the Bible (see p. 28)?
7. How is one nourished by Scripture and doctrine (see p. 28)?
8. Rather than being just a good communicator, what should a preacher be able to do (see p. 28)?
9. How had Timothy been nourished in Scripture in the past (see p. 29)?
10. Describe the kind of teaching that a servant of God should avoid (see p. 31).
11. What kind of mind should a spiritual leader have (see p. 31)?
12. What kind of discipline preoccupied many in the ancient Greek world? In contrast, what kind of training did Paul exhort Timothy to pursue (vv. 7-8; see p. 33)?
13. In what realm is the greatest benefit of discipline achieved? Explain (see p. 34).
14. What did the phrase "a faithful saying" (v. 9) introduce in the early church (see p. 35)?
15. What means of grace does a servant of God employ in pursuing godliness (see p. 35)?

Pondering the Principles

1. William Tyndale's commitment to knowing and understanding God's Word made an unprecedented impact on the English-speaking world. In spite of his imprisonment and the risk to his life, he continued with his personal study and translation of the Bible. Evaluate your desire to know the Word in light of Tyndale's example. Does your Bible sit on a shelf and collect dust, or is it an active part of your spiritual growth? How are you letting God's Word teach, correct, and train you in righteous living (2 Tim. 3:16-17)?

2. A pastor has a hard enough job disciplining himself for godliness, let alone diligently studying Scripture to instruct his congregation and warn them about doctrinal error. Hebrews 13:17 says, "Obey them that have the rule over you, and submit yourselves; for they watch for your souls, as they that must give account, that they may do it with joy, and not with grief; for that is unprofitable for you." Pray that God would raise up many faithful men and women in your church who can assist your pastor in serving God by ministering to others (Eph. 4:12). Encourage your pastor often and set an example with an obedient and submissive spirit. And be ready to share material things with those who teach you spiritual truths (Gal. 6:6).

3. Evaluate your level of discipline in the physical and spiritual realms. Although a measure of physical exercise is important for your physical and emotional health, are you preoccupied with it to the extent that you have no time available to develop a godly character? Are you an example of godliness to other believers? If not, determine what steps you must take to become more spiritually fit. Memorize 1 Timothy 4:7b-8: "Discipline yourself for the purpose of godliness; for bodily discipline is only of little profit, but godliness is profitable for all things, since it holds promise for the present life and also for the life to come" (NASB).

3
Qualities of an Excellent Servant—Part 2

Outline

Review
I. The Excellent Servant Warns People of Error (v. 6a)
II. The Excellent Servant Is an Expert Student of Scripture (v. 6b)
III. The Excellent Servant Avoids the Influence of Unholy Teaching (v. 7a)
   A. A Contradiction of the Truth
   B. A Commitment to the Truth
     1. 1 Timothy 6:2-5
     2. Philippians 4:8
     3. 2 Timothy 2:16
     4. Titus 2:15
IV. The Excellent Servant Disciplines Himself in Personal Godliness (vv. 7b-9)
   A. The Exhortation (v. 7b)
     1. "Exercise"
     2. "Godliness"
       a) Its secular use
       b) Its spiritual use
         (1) 1 Timothy 2:2
         (2) 2 Peter 3:11
   B. The Explanation (v. 8)
   C. The Exhortation (v. 9)

Lesson
V. The Excellent Servant Is Committed to Hard Work (v. 10)
   A. The Price of Ministry (v. 10a)
     1. The motives
       a) Knowledge of future rewards
       b) Knowledge of impending judgment

Review

The key phrase of 1 Timothy 4:6-16 is a portion of verse 6, which says, "Thou shalt be a good minister of Jesus Christ." If the servant of Christ is to be what God wants him to be, what the ministry demands him to be, and what the people need him to be, he must measure his life against the right standard.

Seventeenth-century Puritan John Owen wrote that a minister may fill his pews, his communion roll, and the mouths of the public, but what he is on his knees in secret before almighty God is all that he is and no more. What God demands of those serving in ministry goes beyond ability and giftedness to character. What kind of person are you before God? Someone said that personality is what you are in the light when everyone can see, but character is what you are in the dark when no one can see.

Paul wanted Timothy—and anyone else who serves others—to realize that personal virtue is inviolably linked to effectiveness in ministry. God wants men of character.

What are the qualifications? We have looked at four, and we'll look at two more in this chapter.

I. THE EXCELLENT SERVANT WARNS PEOPLE OF ERROR (v. 6a; see pp. 25-27)

"If thou put the brethren in remembrance of these things."

II. THE EXCELLENT SERVANT IS AN EXPERT STUDENT OF SCRIPTURE (v. 6b; see pp. 27-30)

"Nourished up in the words of faith and of good doctrine, unto which thou hast attained."

III. THE EXCELLENT SERVANT AVOIDS THE INFLUENCE OF UNHOLY TEACHING (v. 7a)

"Refuse profane and old wive's fables."

A. A Contradiction of the Truth (see p. 31)

B. A Commitment to the Truth (see pp. 31-32)

1. 1 Timothy 6:2-5—Paul said to Timothy, "These things teach and exhort. If any man teach otherwise, and consent not to wholesome words, even the words of our Lord Jesus Christ, and to the doctrine which is according to godliness, he is proud, knowing nothing, but doting about questions and disputes of words, of which cometh envy, strife, railings, evil suspicions, perverse disputings of men of corrupt minds, and destitute of the

41

truth, supposing that gain is godliness; from such with-draw thyself." The excellent servant shouldn't get involved in unholy teaching. All it does is create suspicion about the Word of God.

2. Philippians 4:8—The excellent servant should be committed to the principle: "Whatever things are true, whatever things are honest, whatever things are just, whatever things are pure, whatever things are lovely, whatever things are of good report; if there be any virtue, and if there be any praise, think on these things." He is not double-minded (James 1:6-8); he is totally committed to the truth of God. That in itself creates strength.

3. 2 Timothy 2:16—Paul told Timothy to "shun profane and vain babblings; for they will increase unto more ungodliness. And their word will eat as doth a gangrene."

4. Titus 2:15—The excellent servant should "speak, and exhort, and rebuke with all authority" that which pertains to the gospel.

The excellent servant feeds on holy truth and avoids anything that might corrupt his pure mind and divert him from pursuing the things of God.

IV. THE EXCELLENT SERVANT DISCIPLINES HIMSELF IN PERSONAL GODLINESS (vv. 7b-9)

"Exercise thyself rather unto godliness. For bodily exercise profiteth little, but godliness is profitable unto all things, having promise of the life that now is, and of that which is to come. This is a faithful saying and worthy of all acceptance."

A. The Exhortation (v. 7b)

It is axiomatic that spiritual exercise for godliness is far more important than physical exercise. Therefore, we are to be devoted to attaining personal godliness.

1. "Exercise" (see pp. 32-34)

2. "Godliness"

a) Its secular use

The Greek word translated "godliness" is *eusebeia*. It was used by ancient philosophers and religionists. The Platonic definition was right conduct regarding the gods. The Stoic definition was knowledge of how God should be worshiped. Lucian, a Greek writer of the second century A.D., said it described one who was a lover of the gods. Greek historian Xenophon said that a godly person was wise concerning the gods. In its pagan usage *eusebeia* referred to a reverence for things that are holy and a preoccupation with matters related to deity. (For documentation see Richard Chenevix Trench's *Synonyms of the New Testament* [Grand Rapids: Eerdmans, 1973], pp. 172-73.)

b) Its spiritual use

In terms of the Christian faith *eusebeia* also refers to a right attitude toward God and a preoccupation with what is holy. Godliness is the highest of all virtues. If the highest attribute of God is His holiness, then the greatest pursuit of mankind is to attain Godlike holiness. Godliness is the heart and soul of spiritual character.

Godliness is said to be at the heart of truth (1 Tim. 6:3). It comes through Christ (2 Pet. 1:3), yet we still must pursue it (1 Tim. 6:11). It brings trouble from a hostile environment (2 Tim. 3:12). And it blesses us eternally—but not necessarily with temporal prosperity (1 Tim. 6:5-8).

(1) 1 Timothy 2:2—We are to "lead a quiet and peaceable [life] in all godliness and honesty."

(2) 2 Peter 3:11—Peter asked, "What manner of persons ought ye to be in all holy living and godliness?" We are to live lives that show respect for God, His Word, and His will. And it starts at home (1 Tim. 5:4).

B. The Explanation (v. 8; see pp. 34-35)

C. The Exhortation (v. 9; see pp. 35-36)

Lesson

V. THE EXCELLENT SERVANT IS COMMITTED TO HARD WORK (v. 10)

Having called us to be godly, Paul now brings us back to earth. The ministry is a heavenly pursuit, but it is also an earthly task—it's hard work.

A. The Price of Ministry (v. 10a)

"We both labor and suffer reproach [strive]."

Since we know that godliness has "promise of the life that now is, and of that which is to come" (v. 8), we labor and strive. We work hard because we realize that what we do has eternal implications. The Greek verbs translated "labor" and "suffer reproach" refer to extreme hard work.

1. The motives

In 2 Corinthians 5:9 Paul says, "We labor that, whether present or absent, we may be accepted of him." Then Paul gives two reasons for working hard.

a) Knowledge of future rewards

In verse 10 Paul says, "We must all appear before the judgment seat of Christ." We will stand before Christ and be eternally rewarded for the service we've rendered Him. The reward we receive will be commensurate with the service we have rendered Christ, whether good or useless (cf. 1 Cor. 3:11-15).

b) Knowledge of impending judgment

In verse 11 Paul says, "Knowing, therefore, the terror of the Lord, we persuade men." Here Paul is looking beyond himself to unregenerate people. They won't experience a time of reward; they'll face judgment. And since we know that, we should persuade them with the truths of the gospel in hopes that through salvation they might avoid judgment.

Paul worked hard because he knew his effort had eternal consequences—reward for himself and the possibility of changing the destiny of unbelievers. That is the perspective that propels the servant of God. There is an eternal heaven and an eternal hell. Everyone on the face of the earth will spend eternity in one place or the other. When we realize that, we are compelled to serve Christ. No one with a reasonable understanding of heaven's glory and hell's horror could ever be mediocre in the ministry unless he had a cold heart. Henry Martyn, the nineteenth-century English missionary to India and Persia, said he wanted to burn out for God. He was inspired by the example of David Brainerd, who died in his late twenties taking the gospel to American Indians. Both of those men gave of themselves because the work needed to be done, and eternity was the issue. We're engaged in an eternal work; the destiny of souls is at stake.

2. The meaning

In verse 10 Paul is probably referring to his companions, including Timothy, when he says, "*We* both labor and suffer reproach" (emphasis added). "Labor" (Gk., *kopiaō*) means "to work to the point of weariness." "Suffer reproach" (Gk., *agōnizomai*) means "to agonize in a struggle." We work to the point of weariness and exhaustion, often in pain, because we understand our eternal objectives.

J. Oswald Sanders wrote, "If he is unwilling to pay the price of fatigue for his leadership, it will always be mediocre" (*Spiritual Leadership* [Chicago: Moody, 1980], p. 175). He also said, "True leadership always exacts a heavy toll on the whole man, and the more effective the leadership is, the higher the price to be paid" (p. 169). We will not mitigate that price because we understand the urgency of our ministry. Weariness, loneliness,

struggle, rising early, staying up late, and forgoing pleasures all come with excellence.

a) Galatians 6:14—Paul said that by taking up the cross
of Christ, he crucified himself to the world—he died
to everything around him and became consumed with
the gospel of Christ.

b) 1 Corinthians 9:16, 26-27—Paul said, "Necessity is
laid upon me; yea, woe is unto me, if I preach not the
gospel! . . . So fight I, not as one that beateth the air;
but I keep under my body, and bring it into subjection." That describes Paul's tremendous effort and
commitment to a ministry with eternal consequences.
In 2 Corinthians 11:24-27 Paul tells of the many times
he was beaten with rods and a whip, and endured
weariness, suffering, pain, agony, and shipwreck.
He endured all those perils because he was totally
committed to the ministry at hand. Why? Because he
had eternity in view. He realized that the destiny of
souls hung in the balance.

B. The Hope of Ministry (v. 10*b*)

"Because we trust in the living God."

The Greek text says, "We have set our hope on the living
God." The phrase "have set our hope" is in the perfect
tense, which means that we did it in the past and continue
to do it in the present. We continually hope in God.

1. A contrast to dead idols

The Old Testament frequently contrasts the living God
with dead idols (1 Sam. 17:26; 2 Kings 19:4, 16; Psalm
42:2; 84:2). All the so-called gods of the nations are actually dead idols. When people serve the gods of this
world, they may perceive themselves as receiving some
temporal, innate reward. Only in that manner can dead
idols have any meaning. But dead idols can't carry anyone beyond the grave because they are dead. We serve
the living God who can and will reward us eternally.

2. A commitment to a living God

We live in hope of the future. Missionaries who preach the gospel of Jesus Christ through the years deprive themselves of many earthly pleasures because their hope is set on the living God. They believe He will provide life for them beyond this life. We're not trying to amass a fortune here so that we can indulge ourselves before we leave. Our hope is set on the future.

a) Romans 8:24—Paul said, "We are saved by hope."

b) 1 Corinthians 4:2-5—Paul said, "It is required in stewards, that a man be found faithful. But with me it is a very small thing that I should be judged of you, or of man's judgment. . . . Judge nothing before the time, until the Lord come, who both will bring to light the hidden things of darkness, and will make manifest the counsels of the hearts; and then shall every man have praise of God." Paul wasn't looking for human praise; he was waiting for God's eternal reward.

As Paul looked to the future, that caused him to serve with his whole heart, striving in the work of the ministry. We hope in an eternal, living God, who will some day reward those who faithfully serve Him.

C. The Affirmation of Ministry (v. 10*c*)

"Who is the Savior of all men, specially of those that believe."

In what sense is God the Savior of all men? How is He specially the Savior of those who believe? Many suggestions have been made. The key to interpreting this phrase is to stay within its context.

The God whom we serve and have set our hope on will one day bring us to full glory. All our sacrifices and labor are eternally worthwhile. But what is our affirmation that God "is the Savior of all men, specially of those that believe"?

1. The universal-salvation interpretation

   a) The concept

   Some people believe that verse 10 teaches universalism—that ultimately everyone will be saved. They believe that all things will be resolved in Christ and that there is no eternal hell.

   b) The contradiction

   We know verse 10 can't be interpreted that way because the Bible doesn't teach that all people will be saved. We believe in *analogia scriptura*, which means that Scripture is always analogous to itself—it doesn't contradict itself. Since God is the author of it all, it is consistent.

   And Scripture teaches that there is an eternal hell. It is a place where the "worm dieth not, and the fire is not quenched" (Mark 9:44, 46, 48). It is eternal just as heaven is eternal. It is the place where the unsaved are set apart from the presence of God forever (Rev. 21:8). It is a place of weeping and gnashing of teeth (Matt. 8:12). It is a place of evil, torment, isolation, and loneliness, separate from the presence of God. Jesus said to the religious hypocrites, "Where I go, ye cannot come" (John 8:21). He was telling them that their ultimate destiny was away from the presence of God.

   There is an eternal hell and separation from God for those who reject the Lord Jesus Christ. So 1 Timothy 4:10 can't be teaching that all people will be saved in a soteriological sense. Second Thessalonians 1:9 says that unbelievers will be "punished with everlasting destruction from the presence of the Lord, and from the glory of his power." So the phrase "God is the Savior of all men" does not mean that all people ultimately will be saved, because that would contradict Scripture.

2. The potential/actual-salvation interpretation

This view states that God is potentially the Savior of all people but actually the Savior of those who believe. That's a true statement. The death of Jesus Christ was powerful enough to pay for the sins of the whole world and deliver all people from their sin (1 John 2:2). However, even though that statement is biblical, I prefer another interpretation of 1 Timothy 4:10.

3. The temporal/eternal-salvation interpretation

   a) The concept

   We do not need to limit the Greek word here translated "Savior" (*sōtēr*) to mean only salvation from sin.

   (1) The use of "Savior" in the Old Testament

   These texts use the Old Testament equivalent of *sōtēr*:

   (*a*) Judges 3:9—Othniel, a judge, is called a savior or deliverer because he delivered the children of Israel from the hands of the king of Mesopotamia.

   (*b*) 2 Kings 13:5—God gave Israel a human savior to deliver them out of the hands of the Syrians.

   (*c*) Nehemiah 9:27—God gave Israel "saviors, who saved them out of the hand of their enemies" (cf. Obad. 21).

   In a general sense the word *savior* means "deliverer" or "sustainer." Gideon and David are both seen as saviors (Judg. 6:14; 2 Sam. 3:18).

   (2) The use of "Savior" in the New Testament

   When Paul preached to the learned men of Athens on Mars' Hill, he said that God is not "worshiped with men's hands, as though he needed anything, seeing he giveth to all life, and breath, and all things . . . for in him we live, and move, and have our being. . . . For we are also his offspring" (Acts 17:25, 28). In a general sense God is the provider and sustainer of life for all people. *Sōtēr* can mean "sustainer," "provider," or "deliverer."

(a) Acts 27:34—During a storm at sea Paul said to the crew, "Take some food; for this is for your health." The Greek word normally translated "salvation" is here translated "health." Paul wasn't talking about spiritual salvation but physical health.

(b) Acts 4:9—After Peter and John healed a man, Peter said, "If we this day be examined of the good deed done to the impotent man, by what means he is made well." Here the Greek word most often translated "save" is translated "made well."

(c) James 5:15—James said, "The prayer of faith shall *save* the sick" (emphasis added).

So the Greek words translated "salvation" or "save" aren't limited to describing the salvation of the soul. They can speak of deliverance from disease or trouble or of sustenance from food.

That is the analogy Paul is using in 1 Timothy 4:10. We have seen God's sustaining and providing power on a worldwide basis. We have seen His great temporal provision for all people. But that provision is especially glorious for the believer because it is not only temporal but also eternal.

God was the Savior of Israel in a temporal sense, but He is the Savior of only a few Jewish people in a spiritual sense. In 1 Corinthians 10:1-5 Paul says, "I would not that ye should be ignorant, that all our fathers were under the cloud, and all passed through the sea, and were all baptized unto Moses in the cloud and in the sea; and did all eat the same spiritual food; and did all drink the same spiritual drink. . . . But with many of them God was not well pleased." God provides sustenance on a temporal level for all, but eternal salvation comes only for those who believe. The nation of Israel left Egypt and eventually entered Canaan. God sustained the existence of the nation by providing them with food and water and delivering them from illness, danger, and enemies. He preserved the nation for many years, yet redeemed only those who believed in Him.

b) The conviction

Paul's argument is this: we labor and strive in the ministry because we believe the consequences are eternal. We have set our hope on a living God, and we know He will save the souls of those who believe because we have seen His sustaining power at work in the world. That's why we work hard. We see beyond the temporal to the eternal consequences. If you ever lose sight of that then you'll lose out in your ministry. We're to serve with all our heart. That's why Paul endured what he did, and that's why any faithful, excellent servant endures what he does. He has set his hope on an eternal God who has proved He can sustain life.

(1) Of Thomas Cochrane

I remember reading about a man named Thomas Cochrane as he was being interviewed for the mission field. He was asked, "What portion of the field do you feel yourself specially called to?" He answered, "I only know I wish it to be the hardest you could offer me." The Lord's work is not for people who are looking for ease and comfort. Yet it is eternally rewarding for those who set their hope on eternity.

(2) Of Richard Baxter

Seventeenth-century English Puritan Richard Baxter wrote that the ministerial work "must be managed laboriously and diligently, being of such unspeakable consequence to others and ourselves. We are seeking to uphold the world, to save it from the curse of God, to perfect the creation, to attain the ends of Christ's redemption, to save ourselves and others from damnation, to overcome the devil, and demolish his kingdom, and set up the kingdom of Christ, and attain and help others to the kingdom of glory. And are these works to be done with a careless mind or a slack hand? Oh see then that this work be done with all your might! Study hard, for the well is deep, and our brains are shallow" (*The Reformed Pastor* [London: James Nisbet, 1860], pp. 164-65).

Our whole work is a labor—but not human labor. Paul said his goal was to "present every man perfect in Christ Jesus" (Col. 1:28). Then he said, "For this I also labor [Gk., *kopiao*, "agonize"], striving according to his working, which worketh in me mightily" (v. 29). Our work isn't performed in the flesh. I work hard, and I can sense that my energy comes from a source beyond myself. I can't explain what I do. If I endeavored to perform my ministry in the flesh, I couldn't do it. My children have said to me, "When you preach, you're interesting; but when you talk, you're nothing special." I can't explain the difference. But I do know that the Spirit of the Lord energizes those who serve Him. We must carry on the work with an awareness of our own insufficiency and our dependence on Christ.

VI. THE EXCELLENT SERVANT TEACHES WITH AUTHORITY (v. 11)

"These things command and teach."

Someone told me about an individual who flunked out of the police academy because he didn't have an authoritative voice. I said, "What does that have to do with being a policeman?" He replied, "You can't go up behind some guy and say in a high-pitched voice, 'Stick 'em up! You're under arrest.' " A policeman has to convey a sense of authority to be effective. That's important in the ministry as well.

A. The Power of Authority

The Greek word translated "teach" in verse 11 refers to passing on information, in this case passing on instruction or doctrine. It is to be done in the form of a command.

1. Its absence in the present

There is much popular, entertainment-oriented preaching today, but not much that is powerful or transforming in nature. Are the weak suggestions coming from the pulpit these days really what God wants? According to Acts 17:30, God "commandeth all men everywhere to repent." When did we decide that was only a suggestion?

2. Its abundance in the past

We are to be in a command mode. We are to teach with gentleness, meekness, and love; yet also with a certain amount of authority and assertiveness.

a) The authority of Christ

Matthew 7:28-29 says, "It came to pass, when Jesus had ended these sayings [the Sermon on the Mount], the people were astonished at his doctrine; for he taught them as one having authority."

b) The authority of Paul

Paul told Timothy many times to be authoritative. In 1 Timothy 1:3 he says, "Charge some that they teach no other doctrine." Then he said, "These things command" (5:7). In 5:20 Paul talks about rebuking people publicly. Then in 6:17 he gives commands to rich people. In Titus 2:15 he says, "These things speak, and exhort, and rebuke with all authority. Let no man despise thee." That doesn't mean we are to be abusive or ungracious. But we are to confront people when they are in flagrant disobedience of God's Word. Somehow we have lost that approach. Paul was often in a command mode. He exhibited mo-

53

ments of tenderness and compassion, but in no way did he mitigate the demand to obey Scripture.

The faithful servant is bold. He challenges sin head on. He confronts unbelief, disobedience, and lack of commitment. God said of Jesus, "This is my beloved Son . . . hear ye him" (Matt. 17:5). The excellent servant carries on that directive, commanding all people to repent and listen to Jesus Christ.

B. The Foundation of Authority

Our authority has a foundation. First, you must know what you believe about the Bible. If you're not sure that it's the Word of God, you won't be authoritative. Next you have to know what God's Word says. If you're not sure what it means, you can't be authoritative. Then you must be concerned about communicating it properly because you care that His Word be upheld. Finally, you should care about people's response to His Word. Authority is built on that foundation. If you have a weak foundation, you won't communicate with authority.

Our teaching should be filled with commands, not just sentimental pleadings. Instead of trying to sneak up on people with God's truth, we need to speak forth the Word of God and let it do its work. An excellent servant speaks with authority.

Focusing on the Facts

1. What does God demand of those who serve in ministry (see p. 41)?
2. To what principle should the excellent servant be committed (see p. 42)?
3. How did the ancient philosophers and religionists define *eusebeia* (see p. 43)?
4. What is the heart and soul of spiritual character (see p. 43)?
5. What two things motivate the excellent servant to work hard? Explain (see p. 44).
6. Define *kopiaō* and *agōnizomai* (see p. 45).
7. Describe Paul's commitment to ministry (1 Cor. 9:16, 26-27; see p. 46).

8. Explain the phrase "we trust in the living God" (1 Tim. 4:10; see p. 46).
9. Describe the universal-salvation interpretation of 1 Timothy 4:10. How is that interpretation contradicted (see pp. 47-48)?
10. What will hell be like for the unsaved (see p. 48)?
11. Describe the potential/actual-salvation interpretation of 1 Timothy 4:10 (see p. 48).
12. Describe the temporal/eternal-salvation interpretation (see p. 49).
13. What can the Greek words translated "salvation" and "save" refer to (see pp. 49-50)?
14. In what way was God the Savior of the nation of Israel (1 Cor. 10:1-5; see p. 50)?
15. Why does the excellent servant work hard (see p. 51)?
16. Although the excellent servant should work hard, what is the source of his work (Col. 1:29; see p. 52)?
17. According to 1 Timothy 4:11 in what manner should the excellent servant teach? Explain (see pp. 52-53).
18. What is the foundation of the servant's authority (see pp. 53-54)?

Pondering the Principles

1. Read Philippians 4:8. The excellent servant should be committed to dwelling on the things in that verse. Make a list of each attribute listed in Philippians 4:8. Next to each one, list the things that fall under that attribute. For example, under the attribute *pure* you might list those TV programs you know are pure in their content. You might also want to make a separate list of that which is opposite as a reminder to avoid them. Whenever you are confronted with something new, evaluate it in light of Philippians 4:8 and your list.

2. What kind of commitment are you willing to make to the ministry of Jesus Christ? Are you willing to be as committed as Paul, who risked his life in service to Christ? Or will you risk none of your comfort and possessions so that you can maintain your unthreatened life-style? Perhaps your commitment to Christ lies somewhere between those two. Examine it in light of Matthew 16:24-26. What should your commitment be? What do you need to do to make good on that commitment?

3. Review the section on the foundation of authority (see pp. 53-54). Do you have a strong foundation to draw on when you teach God's truth to someone else? Do you believe the Bible is the complete Word of God? Do you know how to interpret God's Word? Do you know what it means by what it says? Can you communicate it so others understand what you are saying? When you teach others, are you legitimately concerned that they practice what they have been taught? If you are weak in any of those areas, strengthen them by strengthening your commitment to God's Word. Consult your local Christian bookstore or church library about books on the Bible itself. Learn why it is reasonable to believe that the Bible is God's inerrant Word. Also, take advantage of the various Bible study tools available in order to become more proficient in interpreting the Bible. The better you understand God's Word, the better you will be able to communicate it. Finally, examine your attitude regarding others. Do you truly seek that they might grow in Christ? Have the same goal that Paul reflects in Colossians 1:28. Thank the Lord for the provision of His Word.

4
Qualities of an Excellent Servant—Part 3

Outline

Introduction

Review
I. The Excellent Servant Warns People of Error (v. 6a)
II. The Excellent Servant Is an Expert Student of Scripture (v. 6b)
III. The Excellent Servant Avoids the Influence of Unholy Teaching (v. 7a)
IV. The Excellent Servant Disciplines Himself in Personal Godliness (vv. 7b-9)
V. The Excellent Servant Is Committed to Hard Work (v. 10)
VI. The Excellent Servant Teaches with Authority (v. 11)
   A. The Power of Authority
   B. The Foundation of Authority

Lesson
VIII. The Excellent Servant Is a Model of Spiritual Virtue (v. 12)
   A. The Power of an Exemplary Life
      1. Defined
      2. Described
      3. Demanded
   B. The Pursuit of Ecclesiastical Respect
      1. The disadvantage of youth
      2. The advantage of godliness
         a) In word
            (1) Raising the standard
               (a) Our speech is to be truthful
               (b) Our speech is to be gracious
               (c) Our speech is to be pure
            (2) Lowering the standard

b) In conduct
   (1) Insights into a righteous life-style
   (2) Injunctions for a righteous life-style
c) In love
   (1) Sacrificing yourself
   (2) Meeting the needs of others
      (a) The example of Paul
      (b) The example of Epaphroditus
d) In faith
e) In purity

Conclusion

Introduction

An Interview on Policing the Ministry

A few years ago I was asked to participate in a television program with a local network affiliate. They wanted to add a little religious flavor to their program, so they asked me if I would do an interview with a well-known local newscaster. In his attempt to identify where I fit into the evangelical framework, he went through a list of media preachers to determine whom I was most comparable to. I said I wasn't like any of the people he named. Then he asked me to explain the emphasis of our ministry. I told him we teach the Word of God and work within the framework of a church. Then he asked, "Do the things other preachers do to raise money bother you, especially those who indulge their own desire for wealth?" I told him they did. He asked, "Why don't you do something about it? How can so many people who call themselves Christians do the kinds of things you feel misrepresent what you believe?" Then he added, "Who is in charge of your movement?"

That was an insightful question. I said, "From a human viewpoint, no one's in charge. But there is a standard that all of us who minister ought to be measured against, and that standard is the Bible. Admittedly, there are people who do not hold their lives or ministries against that standard." Then he asked an equally insightful question: "Why don't you police your movement? It's giving you bad press. The negative attitude about Christian ministers and ministry appears to have resulted because some ministers have abused the biblical standard." I told him I'd be happy to police people in ministry—I just didn't know how to pull it off. Fortunately, I know that ultimately God will deal with every violation.

Can we police our movement? We can when we use the Word of God as the standard. We should measure every ministry and every man in ministry by it—and we have the right to do so.

Review

I. THE EXCELLENT SERVANT WARNS PEOPLE OF ERROR (v. 6a; see pp. 25-27)

"If thou put the brethren in remembrance of these things, thou shalt be a good minister of Jesus Christ."

II. THE EXCELLENT SERVANT IS AN EXPERT STUDENT OF SCRIPTURE (v. 6b; see pp. 27-30)

"Nourished up in the words of the faith and of good doctrine, unto which thou hast attained."

Not long ago I spent two days with a Christian layman. He gave me a paper he had recently written on the rapture of the church in relation to the sequence of events in the end times. The paper was about thirty pages long, single spaced. He said, "I spent three-hundred-and-fifty hours studying this particular theme so that I might understand the Word of God better." Here was a busy man who managed many corporations, yet he committed 350 hours to study one biblical issue. I know men in the ministry who have never spent 350 hours on any issue in Scripture! That layman is an excellent servant of Jesus Christ and an expert student of Scripture.

III. THE EXCELLENT SERVANT AVOIDS THE INFLUENCE OF UNHOLY TEACHING (v. 7a; see pp. 31-32, 41-42)

"Refuse profane and old wives' fables."

IV. THE EXCELLENT SERVANT DISCIPLINES HIMSELF IN PERSONAL GODLINESS (vv. 7b-9; see pp. 32-34, 42-43)

"Exercise thyself rather unto godliness. For bodily exercise profiteth little, but godliness is profitable unto all things, having promise of the life that now is, and of that which is to come. This is a faithful saying and worthy of all acceptance."

V. THE EXCELLENT SERVANT IS COMMITTED TO HARD WORK (v. 10; see pp. 44-52)

"We both labor and suffer reproach [strive], because we trust in the living God, who is the Savior of all men, specially of those that believe."

VI. THE EXCELLENT SERVANT TEACHES WITH AUTHORITY (v. 11)

"These things command and teach."

A. The Power of Authority (see pp. 52-53)

B. The Foundation of Authority (see pp. 53-54)

The ability to teach with authority is built on four facts. The first fact is your view of Scripture. If you believe in an inspired and inerrant text, you know God's Word is authoritative. Second, authority is built on your understanding of Scripture. If you don't know what Scripture says, how can you speak it authoritatively? That's why most seminaries teach the principles of hermeneutics (Gk., *hermeneuō*), which means "to explain," "to translate," or "to interpret." You need to understand the principles of interpretation so you can find the meaning of a passage. Sometimes it's only after you study the language, context, culture, geography, and history of a passage that you can interpret it correctly. Anyone who desires to teach must learn those principles so he can be "a workman that needeth not to be ashamed, rightly dividing the word of truth" (2 Tim. 2:15). Third, you will speak with conviction and authority when you understand how urgent it is for people to hear God's Word. And, fourth, you can speak with authority because the Lord commands you to, and you want to be obedient. If those things are in place, you will teach with authority. There will be strength and boldness in your teaching.

Lesson

VII. THE EXCELLENT SERVANT IS A MODEL OF SPIRITUAL VIRTUE (v. 12)

"Let no man despise thy youth, but be thou an example of the believers, in word, in conduct, in love, in spirit, in faith, in purity."

A. The Power of an Exemplary Life

1. Defined

The Greek word translated "example" is *tupos*, which means "model," "image," or "pattern." A dressmaker will lay a pattern on top of material and cut the material to match the pattern. An artist uses a model in order to reproduce its likeness in a painting. When you set an example, you are giving people a pattern to follow. That is at the heart of excellence in ministry. Seventeenth-century Puritan Thomas Brooks said that example is the most powerful rhetoric (*The Complete Works of Thomas Brooks*, vol. 2 [Edinburgh: James Nichol], pp. 169-70). Someone once said, "Your life speaks so loud I can't hear what you say." Your life-style is your most powerful message. Excellent servants need to learn that.

Godliness Versus Academic Credibility

A friend of mine recently visited his alma mater—a well-known seminary in our country. He had noticed that the majority of the graduates appeared to lack an understanding of true godliness. He suggested that they add a class about holiness and godliness in personal life. One of the professors said, "That wouldn't have any academic credibility." But academic credibility is not the main issue in ministry. Give me a godly person, and I'll show you someone you can pattern your life after. Give me a person whose head is full

61

of knowledge but doesn't have any virtue in his life, and I'll show you a person you had better run from. He will confuse you, and you'll begin to act like him, having all the right truth and none of the right behavior. The dichotomy of such a life is deadly and frightening.

2. Described

The single greatest tool of leadership is the power of an exemplary life. In verse 12 Paul says, "Let no man despise [look down on] thy youth, but be thou an example [to] the believers, in word, in conduct, in love, in spirit, in faith, in purity." (The phrase "in spirit" was added in later manuscripts—it doesn't appear in the earlier ones.) We are to be an example in five areas: word, conduct, love, faith, and purity. Authoritative preaching is useless if it isn't backed up by a virtuous life.

A certain man with a television ministry often calls the people who watch his program to godliness. He says that we all need to be committed to the Lord and get our lives right with Him. Yet I know that that man committed adultery, divorced his wife, and ran off with a twenty-year-old woman. Four years later he came back and started his ministry again. Based on the pattern of his life, there's no credibility in what he says. For him to tell people to get right with God is hypocrisy.

Whenever a pattern of godliness is missing from a person's life, the power of his ministry is gone, and it becomes hollow and shallow. I've often heard people say, "So-and-so is such a good preacher; why doesn't anyone go to his church?" Perhaps the people who attended that church have seen that his life doesn't match what he preaches. A loss of integrity is more than any minister can handle. Puritan Thomas Fuller said that though the words of the wise be as nails fastened by the master craftsman, yet their examples are the hammers to drive them in, to take the deeper hold. You can put the nails of truth on the surface of peoples' hearts, but if you want to hammer them deep into their souls, you need to set the pattern.

3. Demanded

The New Testament is replete with injunctions for setting a pattern of godly living. Note these commands from the apostle Paul:

a) 1 Corinthians 4:16—"I beseech you, be ye followers of me." You might believe Paul was being egotistic. He wasn't—he was simply exhibiting the character of a godly man who knew he was to be an example. Now obviously he knew he wasn't perfect, but it was his objective—as much as was humanly possible—to be what the people were to be. No man should aim for less than that and still be in ministry. The Greek word translated "followers" is *mimētēs*, from which the English word *mimic* is derived.

b) 1 Corinthians 10:31, 33; 11:1—"Do all to the glory of God. . . .Even as I please all men in all things, not seeking mine own profit, but the profit of many, that they may be saved. Be ye followers of me, even as I also am of Christ."

c) Philippians 3:17—"Be followers together of me, and mark them who walk even as ye have us for an example."

d) Philippians 4:9—"Those things which ye have both learned, and received, and heard, and seen in me, do."

e) 1 Thessalonians 1:5-6—"Our gospel came not unto you in word only, but also in power, and in the Holy Spirit, and in much assurance, as ye know what manner of men we were among you for your sake. And ye became followers of us, and of the Lord."

f) 2 Thessalonians 3:7, 9—"Ye yourselves know how ye ought to follow us; for we behaved not ourselves disorderly among you . . . but to make ourselves an example unto you to follow us."

g) 2 Timothy 1:13—"Hold fast the form of sound words, which thou hast heard of me."

The author of Hebrews said, "Remember them who have the rule over you, who have spoken unto you the word of God, whose faith follow" (13:7). When you minister in the church, you are to lead a life that others can follow. That's a tremendous challenge, which is why James said, "Be not many teachers, knowing that we shall receive the greater judgment" (James 3:1). It's a serious matter to be guilty of teaching error or living hypocritically. A man's life must match his message. Tragically, that principle is often violated by those in the ministry.

B. The Pursuit of Ecclesiastical Respect

1. The disadvantage of youth

In 1 Timothy 4:12 Paul tells Timothy, "Let no man despise thy youth, but be thou an example [to] the believers." Timothy was young, and was therefore subject to a certain amount of questioning. So Paul told Timothy that he had to be respected if people were to follow him. But since he was young, Timothy would have to earn that respect. In Greek culture, as in other cultures, if a man wasn't aged, he had to earn respect.

How old was Timothy? When he first joined Paul on the second missionary journey (Acts 16:1-3) Timothy was probably in his early to mid twenties. It was then fifteen years later. So he was probably in his late thirties. In the Greek culture, a man in his late thirties was considered youthful. In fact, in Acts 7:58 Luke refers to Paul as a young man at a time when he must have been more than thirty. The Greek word translated "youth" in 1 Timothy 4:12 (*neotēs*) was used to describe anyone up to the age of forty. A man was considered young until he was forty, and then he was deemed mature, skilled, and wise.

Since Timothy was less than forty, Paul encouraged him by telling him not to let anyone look down on, or show contempt for, his youth. How was Timothy going to gain their respect? By being "an example [to] the believers." To offset his youth and gain the respect of his flock, he needed to reveal himself as a model of spiritual virtue.

2. The advantage of godliness

   a) In word

   The conversation of the servant of God is to be exemplary. In Matthew 12:34 Jesus says, "Out of the abundance of the heart the mouth speaketh." Whatever comes out of the mouth reveals what is in a person's heart. That's why Jesus said, "By thy words thou shalt be justified, and by thy words thou shalt be condemned" (v. 37).

   (1) Raising the standard

   Ephesians 4:25-26, 29 tells us what our speech should be like.

   (a) Our speech is to be truthful

   Verse 25 says, "Putting away lying." A servant of the Lord should never speak any falsehood. He shouldn't talk out of both sides of his mouth—telling one thing to one person and another to someone else. Then Paul says, "Speak every man truth with his neighbor" (v. 25). You should speak the truth to everyone. The credibility of a leader is destroyed when people compare notes about the lies he has told them.

   (b) Our speech is to be gracious

   In verse 26 Paul says, "Be ye angry, and sin not." There's a place for holy wrath and righteous indignation, but not for the sin of anger—especially the smoldering kind of anger that lasts into the next day and longer. No excellent servant of Jesus Christ will ever speak words of wrath or anger. He will never reach the point where he is frustrated—so upset that his words are bitter, vengeful, or ungracious. His speech is to "be always with grace, seasoned with salt" (Col. 4:6).

(c) Our speech is to be pure

Verse 29 says, "Let no corrupt communication proceed out of your mouth." The speech of a believer should never be less than pure. It is embarrassing to hear someone who claims to serve Jesus Christ speak ungodly words. That just reveals a dirty heart. There's no place for corrupt or filthy communication in the Christian life.

Speech that glorifies God "is good to the use of edifying, that it may minister grace unto the hearers" (v. 29). There's a place for fun and joy, for "a merry heart doeth good like a medicine" (Prov. 17:22). But there's no place for perverse talk, angry speech, and a lying tongue.

(2) Lowering the standard

Throughout the history of the church there are many illustrations of men who destroyed their credibility through anger. There have been men in the ministry who use double standards. Such people lower the standard of ministry and should be disqualified from serving as a result. Yet many people accept that standard.

Colossians 3:8-9 says, "Put off all these: anger, wrath, malice, blasphemy, filthy communication out of your mouth. Lie not to one another." All those things refer to speech, and none of them should come out of the mouth of any believer, especially someone in spiritual leadership.

b) In conduct

(1) Insights into a righteous life-style

You are to be a model of righteous living—a person who lives out his convictions based on biblical principles. The things you do, the places you go, the things you possess—any aspect of your life is a sermon. That sermon will either contradict or substantiate what you say.

One pastor was given a new Rolls Royce from his church. I suppose they knew he wanted one. The pastor told them to take it back and redo the interior because he didn't like the color! Some ministers are like leeches, sucking blood out of people for their own benefit (cf. Prov. 30:15). Paul said, "I have coveted no man's silver, or gold, or apparel" (Acts 20:33). Paul didn't want anything from people except the opportunity to give his life to them. When you match a man's materialistic life-style with the biblical message he gives, you're left with blatant hypocrisy that undermines everything he has said. A man is what he lives, not what he says. But when a man lives what he says, there is power and authority in his message.

(2) Injunctions for a righteous life-style

If we are to set a style of living that others are to follow, it has to be righteous.

(*a*) James 3:13—"Who is a wise man and endued with knowledge among you? Let him show out of a good life his works with meekness of wisdom." You should follow the person who by example shows you how to live.

(*b*) Hebrews 13:7—"Remember them who have the rule over you, who have spoken unto you the word of God, whose faith follow,

67

considering the end of their manner of life." That kind of life-style will lead you to eternal reward.

(c) 1 Peter 1:15—"As he who hath called you is holy, so be ye holy in all manner of life."

(d) 1 Peter 2:12—"[Have] your behavior honest among the Gentiles, that, whereas they speak against you as evildoers, they may by your good works, which they shall behold, glorify God in the day of visitation." Your life should be so virtuous, honorable, and biblical that your critics have nothing to say against you.

(e) 1 Peter 3:1-2—"Ye wives, be in subjection to your own husbands that, if any obey not the word, they also may without the word be won by the behavior of the wives, while they behold your chaste conduct coupled with fear."

(f) 1 Peter 3:16—"[Have] a good conscience, that, whereas they speak evil of you, as of evildoers, they may be ashamed that falsely accuse your good manner of life in Christ."

The proof of what you say is in how you live, where you go, what you do, and how you spend your money. I'm not saying you should be poor, or that you can't accept what God graciously gives you, but I am saying not to pursue a materialistic life-style. I've been blessed abundantly with tangible gifts. Sometimes I feel bad about that until I consider the source of them. If I can examine my heart and honestly say that I haven't sought any of them, and that God in His grace has chosen to give them, then I can accept them. The issue is attitude. You can have a wrong attitude toward material things even if you don't possess a lot. If you have the desire to possess many things, then your pursuit is wrong, whether you get what you want or not.

Should God choose to bless you, and your heart is right, you will use what He has given you for His glory.

Examining an Incompatible Life-Style

What do you spend your time, money, and energy on? The life-style propagated by the world today is completely incompatible with the standards of Scripture. Many families disintegrate because both spouses want to work so that they can buy bigger houses or bigger cars. They devote what little spare time they have to firming up their bodies instead of building up their souls, their families, or their children. And the church, instead of maintaining an alternative life-style, too often mimics the world's perspectives.

c) In love

(1) Sacrificing yourself

Ministering in love doesn't necessarily mean you're to be a hand-shaker and a back-slapper, although that's part of the fun of the ministry. We have to use a biblical definition of love. Biblical love is self-sacrificing service on behalf of others. Jesus said, "Greater love hath no man than this, that a man lay down his life for his friends" (John 15:13). That's the heart of ministry. God calls us to love His people enough to willingly give up everything in order to strengthen and build up others in the Lord. John 3:16 says, "God so loved the world, that he *gave*" (emphasis added). Anything less than that isn't love. There are givers and takers in this world—the people who truly love are the givers, not the takers.

(2) Meeting the needs of others

(*a*) The example of Paul

Here's a wonderful testimony of Paul's affection for the Thessalonians: "We were gentle among you, even as a nurse cherisheth her children. So, being affectionately desirous of you, we were willing to have imparted unto you, not the gospel of God only but also our own souls, because ye were dear unto us. For ye remember, brethren, our labor and travail; for laboring night and day, because we would not be chargeable unto any of you, we preached unto you the gospel of God. Ye are witnesses, and God also, how holily and justly and unblamably we behaved ourselves among you that believe, as ye know how we exhorted and encouraged and charged every one of you, as a father doth his children, that ye would walk worthy of God" (1 Thess. 2:7-12).

(*b*) The example of Epaphroditus

Epaphroditus nearly died in his service to God's people. Paul said, "He was sick near unto death, but God had mercy on him" (Phil. 2:27). Why did he almost die? "For the work of Christ, he was near unto death, not regarding his life, to supply [others'] lack of service" (v. 30).

Paul said, "If I be offered upon the sacrifice and service of your faith, I joy, and rejoice with you all" (Phil. 2:17). Paul was willing to give up his life. We have only one life to live, so we should live it as God desires.

From time to time I've had the opportunity to visit other churches in the United States and foreign countries. Those visits will spur this question in my mind: Should I stay and spend myself at Grace Church or move on to another ministry? Yet I know God has called me to give my life to the people of this church. That's exactly what I'll continue to do, and that's how my love for the brethren is expressed. We're to offer self-sacrificing service on behalf of others.

d) In faith

The Greek word translated "faith" in 1 Timothy 4:12 could be translated "faithfulness," "trustworthiness," or "consistency." Timothy was to be consistent, faithful, and trustworthy in his ministry. People can follow that kind of leader. In 1 Corinthians 4:2 Paul says, "It is required in stewards, that a man be found faithful." Consistency separates those who succeed from those who fail. Only loyal, trustworthy, and faithful people will serve Christ with unwavering consistency throughout their lives.

Paul had the reputation of being faithful. So did his co-laborers. Epaphras (Col. 1:7) and Tychicus (Col. 4:7) were just two of many faithful servants of Christ.

e) In purity

The Greek word translated "purity" (*hagneia*) refers not only to sexual chastity, but also to the intents of the heart. If your heart is pure, your behavior will be pure as well.

History has shown us that a ministry can be devastated by sexual impurity on the part of its leaders. I believe that men involved in the leadership of the church are vulnerable in that area and must not let down their guard. We all must maintain absolute moral purity. In 2 Timothy 2:22 Paul tells Timothy to flee youthful lusts.

Conclusion

First Timothy 4:12 tells us that if a person is to be an excellent servant of Jesus Christ, he must be a model of virtue in speech, lifestyle, sacrificial love, trustworthiness, and moral purity. Anyone who is not a model in those areas has no business being in the position of spiritual leadership. Why? Because if he lives at a lower level, that's where he sets the standard. The responsibility of a spiritual leader is not to live in isolation from the godly standard but to live according to the standard God has set for every believer. That standard must be maintained.

So how can we raise the unacceptable standard of Christianity in our country? First, men who are disqualified on the basis of 1 Timothy 4:12 ought to leave the ministry and do something else. Perhaps God will bless them and use them if they avoid hypocrisy. Second, we need to reinforce God's standards for pastors across the world. We must police Christianity. Finally, we must train a new generation of young people who are totally committed to that standard. I'm not willing to accept a lower standard. I know the Lord isn't. If we are to maintain His standard, we must begin to measure people by it. If they don't qualify, that must be made known. If they qualify, they must be called to greater holiness in their lives. Then we must raise up young people who are committed to these things. We have to police our movement. We should be just as eager to put the wrong person out as we are to put the right person in.

Focusing on the Facts

1. What should every man in ministry be measured by (see p. 59)?
2. Define "example" as it is used in 1 Timothy 4:12 (see p. 61).
3. What is a believer's most powerful message (see p. 61)?
4. Why is it dangerous to follow someone who is full of knowledge yet doesn't have any virtue in his life (see pp. 61-62)?
5. What is the result when a pattern of godliness is missing from a person's life (see p. 62)?
6. What are some of the injunctions that Scripture gives for setting a pattern of godly living (see pp. 63-64)?
7. In what way was Timothy at a disadvantage in ministry? Explain (see p. 64).
8. How old might Timothy have been when Paul wrote 1 Timothy (see p. 64)?
9. What do a person's words reveal (Matt. 12:34; see p. 65)?
10. According to Ephesians 4:25-26, 29, in what three ways is the speech of the servant of God to be exemplary? Explain each (see pp. 65-66).
11. What is a model of righteous living (see p. 67)?
12. A man is what he _____, not what he _____ (see p. 67).

13. What does Scripture teach us about living a righteous life (see pp. 67-68)?
14. How is the believer to be an example in love (see p. 69)?
15. How did Paul show his love to the Thessalonians (1 Thess. 2:7-12; see pp. 69-70)?
16. Why did Epaphroditus almost die (Phil. 2:30; see p. 70)?
17. What separates those who succeed from those who fail (1 Cor. 4:2; see p. 71)?
18. In what two ways is the excellent servant to be an example in purity (see p. 71)?
19. How can we raise the standard of Christianity in our country (see p. 72)?

Pondering the Principles

1. As Christians, we are exhorted to become knowledgeable of Scripture. Yet we must be careful not to pursue biblical knowledge to the exclusion of living holy lives. Read 1 Peter 1:14-16. According to verses 15-16, why should Christians live holy lives? According to verse 15, who is the model of holiness? What is the best way for believers to know as much as they can about the model of holiness? Based on your answer, what is the main reason for gaining biblical knowledge? As a result, what should be the priority of your life?

2. What are the five areas in which you can be an example to other believers (1 Tim. 4:12; see pp. 65-72)? Are you an example to others in any of those areas at the present time? Give some examples. Are you proving to be a negative example in any of those areas? Again, give some examples. How might you turn those negative examples into positive ones? Seek to be an example in every area, and ask God to grant you the wisdom necessary for doing so.

5
Qualities of an Excellent Servant—Part 4

Outline

Review
I. The Excellent Servant Warns People of Error (v. 6a)
II. The Excellent Servant Is an Expert Student of Scripture (v. 6b)
III. The Excellent Servant Avoids the Influence of Unholy Teaching (v. 7a)
IV. The Excellent Servant Disciplines Himself in Personal Godliness (vv. 7b-9)
V. The Excellent Servant Is Committed to Hard Work (v. 10)
VI. The Excellent Servant Teaches with Authority (v. 11)
VII. The Excellent Servant Is a Model of Spiritual Virtue (v. 12)

Lesson
VIII. The Excellent Servant Has a Thoroughly Biblical Ministry (v. 13)
A. Total Preparation
B. Total Ministry
1. The reading
a) The pattern of the synagogue
(1) Affirmed by Jesus
(a) Standing up to read
(b) Sitting down to exposit
(2) Acknowledged by the Jerusalem Council
b) The pattern of the New Testament church
2. The exhortation
3. The teaching
IX. The Excellent Servant Fulfills His Calling (v. 14)
A. The Pressure of Ministry
B. The Affirmation of Ministry
1. Subjective affirmation

a) Defining the gift
b) Designing the gift
c) Desiring the gift
2. Objective affirmation
3. Collective affirmation

Conclusion

Review

Each portion of Scripture is usually built around a particular theme or emphasis. First Timothy 4:6-16 is no different. The theme of this passage is in a short phrase of verse 6: "Thou shalt be a good minister of Jesus Christ." What does it mean to be an excellent servant of Jesus Christ?

   I. THE EXCELLENT SERVANT WARNS PEOPLE OF ERROR (v. 6*a*; see pp. 25-27)

  II. THE EXCELLENT SERVANT IS AN EXPERT STUDENT OF SCRIPTURE (v. 6*b*; see pp. 27-30)

 III. THE EXCELLENT SERVANT AVOIDS THE INFLUENCE OF UNHOLY TEACHING (v. 7*a*; see pp. 31-32, 41-42)

 IV. THE EXCELLENT SERVANT DISCIPLINES HIMSELF IN PERSONAL GODLINESS (vv. 7*b*-9; see pp. 32-34, 42-43)

  V. THE EXCELLENT SERVANT IS COMMITTED TO HARD WORK (v. 10; see pp. 44-52)

 VI. THE EXCELLENT SERVANT TEACHES WITH AUTHORITY (v. 11; see pp. 52-54, 60-61)

VII. THE EXCELLENT SERVANT IS A MODEL OF SPIRITUAL VIRTUE (v. 12; see pp. 61-72)

Those first seven qualities can be summed up in seven words. The excellent servant who warns people of error is

76

discerning. We are to know the difference between truth and error. The expert student of Scripture has the ability of scholarship. The one who avoids the influence of unholy teaching is separate. We are to set ourselves apart from whatever influences us toward unrighteousness. He who pursues godliness is holy. He who works hard is diligent. He who teaches with authority has power. And he who is a model of spiritual virtue has integrity. Those characteristics mark the person who serves Jesus Christ with excellence. They should be characteristic of all of us.

Lesson

VIII. THE EXCELLENT SERVANT HAS A THOROUGHLY BIBLICAL MINISTRY (v. 13)

"Till I come, give attendance to reading, to exhortation, to doctrine."

A. Total Preparation

The phrase "till I come" implies that Paul was going to return to Ephesus and meet Timothy there again. First Timothy 3:14 attests to that: "These things write I unto thee, hoping to come unto thee shortly." So until Paul returned, he wanted Timothy to give his attention to the reading, the exhortation, and the doctrine (or teaching).

The Greek verb translated "give attendance" is *prosechō*. It is a present active imperative, a continuing command. Paul is commanding Timothy to continually give attention to reading, exhortation, and teaching. It was to become Timothy's way of life. Commentator Donald Guthrie tells us that the verb "implies previous preparation in private" (*The Pastoral Epistles* [Grand Rapids: Eerdmans, 1978], p. 97). The same verb is used in Hebrews 7:13 of the priests who were continually devoted to their service at the altar. So Timothy was to center his ministry on reading, exhortation, and teaching.

B. Total Ministry

1. The reading

In verse 13 a definite article appears in the Greek text before the word translated "reading." Timothy was to give attention to "the reading." In the services of the early church a time was set aside for the reading of Scripture. It was followed by an exposition of the text.

When Paul told Timothy to give attention to the reading, that meant he would have to be careful about the text he selected, in the accuracy of his exposition, and all the matters regarding his preparation.

a) The pattern of the synagogue

The early church drew the pattern for its services from the synagogue.

(1) Affirmed by Jesus

(*a*) Standing up to read

According to Luke 4:15 Jesus had been teaching in the synagogues in Galilee. Verse 16 says, "He came to Nazareth, where he had been brought up; and, as his custom was, he went into the synagogue on the sabbath day, and stood up to read." As a visiting rabbi, He was invited to read a portion of Scripture. Whoever read from Scripture always stood up to read, a custom derived from Nehemiah 8:1-5. After rebuilding the walls of Jerusalem, the people were excited about what God was doing and asked for the law of Moses to be read before them. As Ezra stood to read God's Word, the people stood for the entire length of the reading.

When Jesus stood up to read, "there was delivered unto him the book of the prophet, Isaiah. And when he had opened the book, he found the place where it was written, The

Spirit of the Lord is upon me, because he hath anointed me to preach the gospel to the poor; he hath sent me to heal the brokenhearted, to preach deliverance to the captives, and recovering of sight to the blind, to set at liberty them that are bruised, to preach the acceptable year of the Lord" (Luke 4:17-19). Jesus read a messianic prophecy from Isaiah 61:1.

(b) Sitting down to exposit

Verse 20 says, "He closed the book, and he gave it again to the minister, and sat down." Why did He sit down? Because the custom for teaching in all the synagogues was to be seated. He stood to read; He sat down to explain what He had read. Verses 20-21 say, "The eyes of all them that were in the synagogue were fastened on him. And he began to say unto them, This day is this scripture fulfilled in your ears." That statement was a jolt to the people because He was claiming to be the Messiah. We know He said more than that because verse 22 says they "all bore him witness, and wondered at the gracious words which proceeded out of his mouth."

(2) Acknowledged by the Jerusalem Council

In Acts 15 the Jerusalem Council met to decide how they might avoid offending the Jewish people as a result of their outreach to the Gentiles. They decided to instruct the saved Gentiles to "abstain from pollutions of idols, and from fornication, and from things strangled, and from blood" (v. 20). Verse 21 observes, "For Moses of old time hath in every city them that preach him, being read in the synagogues every sabbath day."

When the people met together in the synagogue, the book of Moses was read and then explained.

That model of expository preaching comes from Nehemiah 8:8: "They read in the book in the law of God distinctly, and gave the sense, and caused them to understand the reading."

b) The pattern of the New Testament church

The New Testament epistles were to be included in such reading and exposition. When the church was founded on the Day of Pentecost, the people "continued steadfastly in the apostles' doctrine" (Acts 2:42). In addition to expositing Old Testament passages, the early church taught the doctrine of the apostles, for it was understood to be the Word of God.

In Colossians 4:16 Paul says, "When this epistle is read among you, cause that it be read also in the church of the Laodiceans, and that ye also read the epistle from Laodicea." There was a time and a place for the reading of the Old Testament. The same became true of the New Testament—the writings of the apostles.

Scripture needs to be explained so that people can understand it. Obviously, the further we are removed culturally, geographically, linguistically, philosophically, and historically from the original text of Scripture, the more necessary it becomes to research those facts. That's the challenge for the Bible teacher and where his effort is needed. If anyone is to give his complete attention to teaching God's Word, he will spend a good portion of his life reconstructing the language, philosophy, geography, culture, and context to make the Word of God understandable. That's why Paul told Timothy to give his complete attention to that task.

2. The exhortation

If the reading and exposition of Scripture tell us what it means, then what is the exhortation all about? It is a call for people to make application. To exhort is to warn people to obey with a view toward judgment.

We are to encourage people to respond properly, telling them about the blessings or the consequences of their actions. We are to explain what the Bible means and then encourage people to apply it. Sometimes exhortation is counsel, sometimes it is comfort, but it is always intended to bind a person's conscience and bring him to a change in behavior.

3. The teaching

The Greek word translated "doctrine" (*didaskalia*) means "teaching." Paul is communicating that the excellent servant gives himself to the process of systematically teaching the Word of God in every dimension of ministry. That embodies the idea of developing a system of theology. It also includes the process of teaching individuals, one-on-one or in small groups.

The systematic teaching of God's Word is a mandate for the church. The church is simply defined in terms of its ministry. I am called to read, explain, and apply the Word of God, and also to give my whole life to the process of teaching it. Our goal is to always minister the Word of God in every dimension of the church's life. We are to disseminate sound teaching to all people at all times through all means. Often the church is diverted from that goal, yet that is the necessary heart and soul of its ministry.

Didaskalia appears fifteen times in the pastoral epistles. That gives us some idea of its importance to the life of the church. No wonder the pastor must be "apt to teach" (1 Tim. 3:2). Since the church's ministry revolves around teaching the Word of God, how could anyone ever hope to lead in a church if he's not a skilled teacher?

When Scripture is read, explained, applied, and lived, the church is succeeding in its ministry. From its earliest years the church has been committed to teaching. In recent times the church has tended to drift into extraneous pursuits. As a result, the Word of God descends lower on the priority list.

Relentless Teachers

First Timothy 5:17 says, "Let the elders that rule well be counted worthy of double honor, especially they who labor in the word and doctrine." The harder a man works in teaching God's Word, the more honorable he is. It's sad to realize that many men in ministry have been diverted into nice pursuits but not the most important one.

We need to be relentless teachers. Puritan clergyman John Flavel wrote, "It is not with us, as with other labourers: They find their work as they leave it, so do not we." Picture the cabinetmaker who leaves his unfinished work and comes back to it as it was the next morning. Flavel continues, "Sin and Satan unravel almost all we do, the impressions we make on our people's souls in one sermon, vanish before the next" (*The Works of John Flavel*, vol. 6 [London: Banner of Truth, 1968], p. 569).

We constantly fight against that unraveling process. That's why we have to be relentless in ministry. And that's why I repeat much of what I teach. Every good pastor and teacher knows that people forget what he teaches. So he must be repetitive. But he also realizes that people become familiar with what he teaches. When they realize they are being taught something they have already heard, they believe they know it and become bored by it. The challenge for the teacher is to repeat his teaching in such a manner that the people believe he is teaching them something new.

It would be easy for me to pack up a hundred sermons, go out on the road, and preach them over and over again. The challenge for me is to stay in the same place, say the same things over and over, yet have people believe I'm teaching them something they've never heard. If you study the Bible, you'll find that Scripture does the same thing. Its principles are repeated over and over in different contexts and through different narratives.

IX. THE EXCELLENT SERVANT FULFILLS HIS CALLING (v. 14)

"Neglect not the gift that is in thee, which was given thee by prophecy, with the laying on of the hands of the presbytery."

There are people who go into the ministry and then bail out because they weren't called there in the first place. But sometimes people who are called into the ministry bail out, and that is a defection from where God intends them to be.

A. The Pressure of Ministry

That Paul says, "Neglect not the gift" (which could be translated "Stop neglecting the gift"), may indicate that Timothy was about to neglect his ministry or had already begun to neglect it. He may even have been close to a point of departure—a point at which people can't handle the internal and external pressure of their situation.

A Look at Timothy's Dilemma

In 2 Timothy 1:3 Paul says, "Without ceasing I have remembrance of thee in my prayers night and day." Paul knew Timothy had a difficult ministry in a hostile environment. The Ephesian church had defected both doctrinally and behaviorally. The church was immoral and aberrant in theology. Paul commissioned Timothy to set things right in the Ephesian church. That was a difficult task for someone Timothy's age, for he was working through his own spiritual development. Here he was faced with formidable foes. The Ephesians in error propounded a high-powered, sophisticated quasi-theology. Paul told Timothy to avoid arguing with them (2 Tim. 2:16, 23).

According to 2 Timothy 1:4 Paul desires to see Timothy, "being mindful of [his] tears." Perhaps Paul had received word that Timothy was experiencing overwhelming grief over his situation. But being reminded of Timothy's true faith (v. 5), he said, "I put thee in remembrance that thou stir up the gift of God, which is in thee by the putting on of my hands" (v. 6). In comparing verse 6 with 1 Timothy 4:14, we know that Paul was one of the elders who laid hands on him.

What ultimately happened to the church at Ephesus? It left its first love and went out of existence (Rev. 2:4-5). Whatever Timothy accomplished there was short-lived. He did everything he could to keep it alive, but the church was dying. He was the best man available, but he was fighting a losing battle. That kind of situation would make any person want to give up. But Paul encouraged Timothy not to become timid and fearful, saying, "God hath not given us the spirit of fear, but of power. . . . Be not thou, therefore, ashamed of the testimony of our Lord, nor of me his prisoner; but be thou partaker of the afflictions of the gospel" (2 Tim. 1:7-8). Timothy had to expect hostility. In verses 12-15 Paul says, "I also suffer these things; nevertheless, I am not ashamed. . . . Hold fast the form of sound words, which thou hast heard of me, in faith and love which is in Christ Jesus. That good thing which was committed unto thee keep by the Holy Spirit, who dwelleth in us. This thou knowest, that all they who are in Asia turned away from me."

In 2 Timothy 2:1 Paul says, "Be strong in the grace that is in Christ Jesus." Paul was trying to strengthen Timothy. In verse 2 he says, "The things that thou hast heard from me among many witnesses, the same commit thou to faithful men, who shall be able to teach others also." Then in verses 3-6 Paul encourages Timothy to be as diligent as a soldier in battle, an athlete in a race, and a farmer planting his field.

Timothy probably experienced some internal pressure as well. Second Timothy 2:22 says, "Flee also youthful lusts." Timothy was not only fighting what appeared to be a losing battle in the church, but also struggling with his own youthful lusts and desires. He may have been questioning his ability to minister for the cause of Christ because of the spiritual battles in his own life. But Paul encouraged him to separate himself from lust and false teaching, and pursue "righteousness, faith, love, peace, with them that call on the Lord out of a pure heart" (v. 22). Paul was trying to get Timothy re-oriented in his ministry.

B. The Affirmation of Ministry

1. Subjective affirmation

In verse 14 Paul tells Timothy that he was gifted for his present ministry by the Holy Spirit. In telling Timothy to fulfill his calling, Paul begins by affirming Timothy's spiritual gift. You can't credit a person for his gift because he doesn't obtain it by his own choice or effort; he is given it by sovereign grace.

a) Defining the gift

The Greek verb translated "neglect not" in verse 14 is a present active imperative. It is a command with a view toward continual behavior. The Greek word translated "gift" is *charisma*, a reference to a gift of grace from God. Every believer is given a gift, which is a means or channel by which the Spirit of God ministers to others. I've been given the gifts of teaching and preaching. Perhaps you have been given the gift of helps, giving, or leadership. Comprehensive lists of all the gifts are in Romans 12 and 1 Corinthians 12, with references in Ephesians 4 and 1 Peter 4.

b) Designing the gift

I like to think of spiritual gifts as divine enablements. They are given to us by the Spirit of God with a sovereign design. The church is made up of many people. It functions like a body, and every person is a part of the body. The spiritual gifts we've been given blend together to enable the body to function properly. For example, Timothy was given a gift for the direct propagation of the Word. That's why Paul told him to teach, preach, command, and exhort. He was to do the work of an evangelist, making full proof of his ministry (2 Tim. 4:5). He was gifted in the areas of evangelism, preaching, teaching, and leadership—all blended together as his own unique spiritual gift.

Each of us has one spiritual gift, a blend of the different gifts the Spirit has put together for each of us. Like a painter who is able to create an infinite number of colors by mixing any combination of the ten or so colors he carries on his palette, so the Spirit of God blends a little of one gift with a little of another to create the perfect combination within you. As a result, you have a unique position in the Body of Christ, with an ability to minister as no one else can.

c) Desiring the gift

No one has ever had to tell me what my gift is. Ever since I committed my life to Christ I've known what God wanted me to do. You receive your gift at salvation, although it may be latent for a while before it flourishes. I can look back and know God has called me to preach and teach—that has always been on my heart. I didn't know how I was going to do it, or if I'd ever be able to do it effectively, but I knew my heart's desire was to teach and preach the Word. And I'm sure that was Timothy's desire as well. When he first met Paul, I know he must have been excited about the possibility of traveling with the greatest of all living preachers. I believe that when God gives us our gift, He includes the faith necessary to operate that gift, which is manifested in the believer's desire to minister.

2. Objective affirmation

In verse 14 Paul says Timothy's gift was given to him by prophecy. That's the objective affirmation of Timothy's call to the ministry. I don't believe he received the gift through the prophecy, but I do believe there was a public affirmation of his gift by direct revelation from God. When did that happen? According to Acts 16:1-3, Paul met Timothy when he was traveling through Derbe and Lystra. Timothy had a good reputation among fellow believers there. He had a wonderful heritage—his mother and grandmother were believers. He came from a Jewish-Gentile background, which made him accessible to both cultures and therefore an ideal man for Paul to take on his journey. Although it is not indicated in Acts 16, I believe it was at that time when a direct prophecy came from God setting aside Timothy to preach and teach the Word. It would have been similar to the event in Acts 13:2 when the Holy Spirit said, "Separate me Barnabas and Saul for the work unto which I have called them." That was a direct revelation, or prophecy, from God to set apart Barnabas and Saul for ministry. After Paul met Timothy it is likely that, as the church came together, the Spirit of God spoke a direct prophecy through one of the prophets, indicating the gift Timothy had received.

I should add that Timothy's experience is not normative. I'm not in the ministry today because God gave me a revelation. Timothy's gift was affirmed in the apostolic era. Today, the objective confirmation would come from providence, not direct revelation. The way God arranges your circumstances and opportunities, and the way He leads and directs people you meet are often the ways He affirms your call. I've had young men ask me if I believe they should go to seminary. One said, "I feel so compelled to preach, but I don't know whether I should go." I said, "Do you have an opportunity to go to seminary?" He said he did. I asked him, "Can you afford to go?" Again he said he did. Then I asked, "Do you have a good seminary you can go to?" Once more he answered in the affirmative. So I said, "Does that sound like the Lord may be arranging the circumstances providentially?" He realized that probably was true. So when you feel compelled to do something, and the opportunity presents itself, that may well be God's providential affirmation.

3. Collective affirmation

The laying on of the hands of the elders is the collective affirmation. The church affirmed Timothy's gift. I'm sure that happened during the time Acts 16:1-3 describes.

When the elders laid hands on Timothy, the church was affirming that Timothy was the right man. Through the voice of a prophet the Holy Spirit affirmed his call. And Timothy's own desire to preach and teach affirmed his calling. That's the way God continues to call people into ministry. The person must first desire to minister. Next there must be the confirmation of the providence of God through circumstances. And finally, a collective assembly of spiritual leaders must put their hands on him, thus recognizing that he is qualified. So Paul encouraged Timothy to fulfill the call of God and not neglect the gift that was confirmed in him.

Spiritual Marathon Ministers

There are many people in ministry who serve for a while then quickly fade away. They're like shooting stars. I'm in awe of those who are faithful to minister the Word of God right to the end of their lives. I call them spiritual marathon ministers. They may have a small congregation, they may be unknown, but they remain faithful and fulfill their calling.

The reason I'm in awe of those people is that I've seen so many bail out of the ministry. That's not to say some of them shouldn't have, because they probably weren't called to the ministry. They may have had good intentions, and they may have served the Lord effectively for a time, but He wanted them in another place. But those who have been called, gifted, and confirmed to be in ministry need to remain there. In Acts 20:24 Paul says, "None of these things [bonds and afflictions] move me, neither count I my life dear unto myself, so that I might finish my course with joy, and the ministry." According to 1 Corinthians 9:27 Paul says his biggest fear is that after having preached to others, he would end up disqualifying himself from ministry.

You'll never be able to evaluate the ministry of John MacArthur until all the evidence is in. The true mark of an excellent servant of Jesus Christ is that he fulfills his calling to the end. He's internally driven by the passion of his heart, and he's externally compelled by the opportunities God has given him and the confirmation of godly men. I remember very well the day I knelt and godly men put their hands on me to set me apart for the ministry. I have a certificate in my office with the names of those who confirmed that I should do the work of the ministry for life. Fulfilling the call is a vital part of being the kind of servant God wants you to be.

Conclusion

The ministry is to be biblical, and the minister is to be a faithful marathon runner. Excellent servants must set an example for the kind of life we're all to live. We're all called to live a biblical life and be students of the Word of God. Each of us should fulfill our giftedness and calling. There are many people in the church who do not study of the Word of God or serve God. They don't know what their gift is because they've never taken advantage of opportunities to be involved in a ministry that might reveal it. Ask yourself: *Where's my ministry? What's my calling? Am I being faithful to it?*

Focusing on the Facts

1. What seven words might you use to describe the first seven qualities of an excellent servant (see pp. 76-77)?
2. Explain the meaning of the verb translated "give attendance" in 1 Timothy 4:13 (see p. 77).
3. What was "the reading" (see pp. 77-78)?
4. What things did Timothy need to be careful about regarding the reading of Scripture (see p. 78)?
5. Explain the pattern of service in the synagogue as illustrated by Luke 4:15-22 (see pp. 78-79).
6. What verse gives a model of expository preaching (see p. 79)?
7. What pattern did the New Testament church follow (see p. 80)?
8. What is the challenge for the Bible teacher (see p. 80)?
9. What is involved in the exhortation of Scripture (see pp. 80-81)?
10. What is involved in the teaching of Scripture (see p. 81)?
11. What should be the goal of the church (see p. 81)?
12. Why do teachers of God's Word need to be relentless (see p. 82)?
13. Why do certain people leave the ministry (see p. 82)?
14. Describe the situation Timothy faced in ministering to the church at Ephesus (see p. 83)?
15. According to 2 Timothy 2:22, what did Paul encourage Timothy to pursue (see p. 84)?
16. What was the subjective affirmation of Timothy's call to the ministry (see p. 84)?
17. Explain how God designs each believer's gift (see p. 85).
18. What was the objective affirmation of Timothy's call to the ministry (see p. 86)?
19. Is Timothy's experience normative for today? Explain (see pp. 86-87).
20. What was the collective affirmation of Timothy's call to the ministry (see p. 87)?

Pondering the Principles

1. Although you may not be called to teach in a church or a ministry, that doesn't alleviate you from the responsibility of learning what God's Word says. As the Bible teacher is challenged to bridge the gap between culture, geography, history, and linguistics, so are you in your own personal study. There are several tools available that can help you. Most commentaries will deal with culture to some degree. Another good source on Bible culture is Alfred Edersheim's *The Life and Times of Jesus the Messiah* (Grand Rapids: Eerdmans, 1980). To learn more about the geography of an area, obtain a good Bible atlas. Good tools for learning about the history of the Bible are a Bible dictionary or *The Zondervan Pictorial Encyclopedia of the Bible* (Grand Rapids: Zondervan, 1976). The hardest aspect for most people is linguistics because they don't know Greek or Hebrew. Helpful tools are W. E. Vine's *An Expository Dictionary of New Testament Words* (Chicago: Moody, 1985) for Greek and *The Theological Wordbook of the Old Testament* (Chicago: Moody, 1980) for Hebrew. (You don't have to know either Greek or Hebrew to use them.) In addition, any good concordance will help you in word study. As you begin to use those tools, your understanding of Scripture will become clearer, and you will begin to know what the Bible means by what it says.

2. The goal of every believer, whether he is called to teach or not, is to remain faithful to Christ until the end of his earthly life. Look up the following verses: Matthew 10:22, 24:45-47, Hebrews 3:14, and Revelation 2:10. What waits for the believer who endures to the end? Based on Hebrews 3:14, what conclusions can you draw from someone who does not remain faithful (cf. 1 John 2:19)? According to Revelation 2:10, what reward does the believer who endures receive? With that in mind, in what manner ought you to live? As you face times of doubt and discouragement in your Christian life or ministry, draw on God's strength, and remember what waits for you at the end of your faithful service.

6
Qualities of an Excellent Servant—Part 5

Outline

Review
I. The Excellent Servant Warns People of Error (v. 6a)
II. The Excellent Servant Is an Expert Student of Scripture (v. 6b)
III. The Excellent Servant Avoids the Influence of Unholy Teaching (v. 7a)
IV. The Excellent Servant Disciplines Himself in Personal Godliness (vv. 7b-9)
V. The Excellent Servant Is Committed to Hard Work (v. 10)
VI. The Excellent Servant Teaches with Authority (v. 11)
VII. The Excellent Servant Is a Model of Spiritual Virtue (v. 12)
VIII. The Excellent Servant Has a Thoroughly Biblical Ministry (v. 13)
IX. The Excellent Servant Fulfills His Calling (v. 14)

Lesson
X. The Excellent Servant Is Totally Absorbed in His Work (v. 15a)
A. The Avoidance of Distractions
B. The Acceptance of Discipline
1. Choosing the post
2. Staying at the post
XI. The Excellent Servant Is Continually Progressing in His Spiritual Growth (v. 15b)
A. By Strenuous Effort
B. By the Spirit's Power

Conclusion
A. The Measure of a Minister (v. 16a)
1. Right conduct
2. Right teaching

B. The Goal of Any Ministry (v. 16b)
1. Perseverance
2. Persuasion

Review

The key statement in 1 Timothy 4 is in verse 6: "Thou shall be a good minister [servant] of Jesus Christ." That is Paul's emphasis; he is calling Timothy to excellence in the ministry. In so doing, he lists eleven qualities of a servant of Christ.

I. THE EXCELLENT SERVANT WARNS PEOPLE OF ERROR (v. 6a; see pp. 25-27)

"If thou put the brethren in remembrance of these things, thou shalt be a good minister of Jesus Christ."

II. THE EXCELLENT SERVANT IS AN EXPERT STUDENT OF SCRIPTURE (v. 6b; see pp. 27-30)

"Nourished up in the words of faith and good doctrine, unto which thou hast attained."

III. THE EXCELLENT SERVANT AVOIDS THE INFLUENCE OF UNHOLY TEACHING (v. 7a; see pp. 31-32, 41-42)

"Refuse profane and old wives' fables."

IV. THE EXCELLENT SERVANT DISCIPLINES HIMSELF IN PERSONAL GODLINESS (vv. 7b-9; see pp. 32-34, 42-43)

"Exercise thyself rather unto godliness. For bodily exercise profiteth little, but godliness is profitable unto all things, having promise of the life that now is, and of that which is to come. This is a faithful saying and worthy of all acceptance."

V. THE EXCELLENT SERVANT IS COMMITTED TO HARD WORK (v. 10; see pp. 44-52)

"Therefore we both labor and suffer reproach, because we trust in the living God, who is the Savior of all men, specially of those that believe."

VI. THE EXCELLENT SERVANT TEACHES WITH AUTHOR-ITY (v. 11; see pp. 52-54, 60-61)

"These things command and teach."

VII. THE EXCELLENT SERVANT IS A MODEL OF SPIRITUAL VIRTUE (v. 12; see pp. 61-72)

"Let no man despise thy youth, but be thou an example of the believers, in word, in conduct, in love, in spirit, in faith, in purity."

VIII. THE EXCELLENT SERVANT HAS A THOROUGHLY BIBLICAL MINISTRY (v. 13; see pp. 77-82)

"Till I come, give attendance to reading, to exhortation, to doctrine."

IX. THE EXCELLENT SERVANT FULFILLS HIS CALLING (v. 14; see pp. 82-88)

"Neglect not the gift that is in thee, which was given thee by prophecy, with the laying on of the hands of the presbytery."

Lesson

X. THE EXCELLENT SERVANT IS TOTALLY ABSORBED IN HIS WORK (v. 15a)

"Meditate upon these things; give thyself wholly to them."

A. The Avoidance of Distractions

Paul exhorts Timothy to be diligent in the things of the ministry and to give himself continually to them. An excellent minister is single-minded, as opposed to the double-minded man, who is unstable in all his ways (James 1:8). His ministry is all consuming. The Greek word translated "meditate" (*meletaō*) conveys the idea of thinking through beforehand—planning, strategizing, or premeditating. When a minister is not doing the work of the ministry, he's planning it. Those are the two things that consume my life; I'm either participating in ministry or planning it. I'm either teaching the Word of God or preparing to teach it.

B. The Acceptance of Discipline

"Give thyself wholly to them" literally reads "be in them" in the Greek text. We're to be wrapped up in ministry—totally absorbed in it. It doesn't take much of a man to be a minister, but it does take all of him. An excellent minister is totally absorbed in his work.

1. Choosing the post

A minister can't have a double agenda. He can't divide his efforts between being in the ministry and becoming a tennis or golf pro, making money, or developing a business on the side. People who fall into that trap never realize their full potential because they have too many things to distract them and drain their energy. A good servant of Christ must bury himself in his ministry, just like Epaphroditus, who nearly died fulfilling his ministry (Phil. 2:25-27). A good minister is to be involved in his ministry, preparing for it, or praying for it.

2. Staying at the post

In 2 Timothy 4:2, Paul tells Timothy to "preach the Word; be instant." Greek scholar Fritz Rienecker tells us that the Greek word translated "instant" (*ephistēmi*) is a military word. It means to stay at your post—to stay on duty (*A Linguistic Key to the Greek New Testament* [Grand Rapids: Zondervan, 1980], p. 647). A servant of God is never off duty; he is always at his post. My dad used to tell me that a preacher ought to be ready to preach, pray, or die at a moment's notice. There's a certain preoccupation in the ministry that never goes away. It is not an insensitivity but a preoccupation. That's as it ought to be, because we are always on duty.

Paul told Timothy to "be instant in season, out of season" (2 Tim. 4:2). A servant of Christ is on duty when it's convenient and when it's not. I went home tired one Sunday night. All I wanted to do was get something cold to drink and sit in a chair and rest. I no sooner sat down than the phone rang. A family was having major problems. I spent forty minutes on the phone, during which time the food my daughter had prepared for me became nearly inedible. As soon as I hung up the phone, it rang again, and it was someone with an even bigger disaster. I suppose that's the Lord's way of letting me know that I'm always on duty. That's how it is in ministry—you have to be totally absorbed in it.

In 2 Timothy 4:5 Paul says to Timothy, "Make full proof of thy ministry." He was to fulfill it, to stick with it, and be consumed by it. A minister who warns his people of error, diligently studies the Word of God, avoids unholy teaching, cultivates a disciplined, holy life, is committed to hard work, teaches with authority, models spiritual virtue, maintains a thoroughly biblical ministry, and fulfills the call of God will of necessity be totally absorbed in the work of the ministry.

XI. THE EXCELLENT SERVANT IS CONTINUALLY PROGRESSING IN HIS SPIRITUAL GROWTH (v. 15b)

"That thy profiting may appear to all."

Paul tells Timothy that his spiritual progress should be obvious to everyone. That implies he hadn't yet reached perfection. A minister should not try to convince his people that he has no flaws but should allow them to see his growth. The standard for a servant of Christ is high, and we all fall short of it. Even Paul said, "Not as though I had already attained . . . I press toward the mark" (Phil. 3:12, 14). Paul had his faults; he wasn't perfect. He lost his temper when the high priest ordered him to be struck in the face, shouting, "God shall smite thee, thou whited wall" (Acts 23:1-5). People need to see our integrity and humility. I'm not perfect, but I hope I'm progressing.

A. By Strenuous Effort

The Greek word translated "profiting" (*prokopē*) is used in a military sense to speak of an advancing force. It was used by the Stoics to refer to advancing in knowledge (Rienecker, p. 628). It was used of a pioneer cutting a trail by strenuous effort and advancing toward a new location. We are to be advancing toward Christlikeness, and we need to let people see that. Rather than trying to convince them we're perfect, we must be honest enough to let them know we're growing.

People sometimes point out to me that what I've said on one tape doesn't agree with what I said on a later tape. My response to them is that I'm growing. I didn't know everything then, and I don't know everything now.

B. By the Spirit's Power

Humanly speaking, no one is fit for the task of ministry. The Lord knows that; the same Lord who gave us these high standards knows that we can never meet them. There's only one answer to that dilemma: when we yield to the Spirit of God and depend on Him for what we can never accomplish on our own, His power will work through us. That's what Paul means when in Colossians 1:29 he says, "For this I also labor, striving according to His working, which worketh in me mightily." It's comforting to know that God, through His Spirit, can make us the servants He wants us to be.

You're Not Off the Hook!

If you're not a pastor, you might be thinking that the qualities of an excellent servant don't apply to you, but they do. Ministers model the behavior that all Christians are to follow. You're to imitate their behavior so that your life will be a pattern for others to follow.

Conclusion

A. The Measure of a Minister (v. 16a)

"Take heed unto thyself and unto the doctrine; continue in them."

"Take heed" means "pay attention." Paul commands Timothy to focus on two things: his conduct and his teaching. Those two things are the heart of the ministry. The eleven qualities we've seen in this passage can be summed up in those two commands.

1. Right conduct

Paul told Timothy, "Take heed unto thyself." He said the same thing to the elders of the Ephesian church (Acts 20:28). The theme of right conduct runs throughout 1 Timothy 4: "nourished up in the words of faith and of good doctrine" (v. 6), "exercise thyself rather unto godliness" (v. 7), "be thou an example" (v. 12), "neglect not the gift that is in thee" (v. 14). Are you an example? Are you training yourself in godliness? Are you being nourished by the Word?

2. Right teaching

This is another theme in 1 Timothy 4: "put the brethren in remembrance of these things" (v. 6), "refuse profane and old wives' fables" (v. 7), "these things command and teach" (v. 11), "till I come, give attendance to reading, to exhortation, to doctrine" (v. 13).

All eleven qualities of an excellent servant of Christ can be reduced to this: concentrate on your own spiritual life and your exposition, exhortation, and application of the Word of God. That is to be the focus of an excellent minister.

B. The Goal of Any Ministry (v. 16b)

"For in doing this thou shalt both save thyself and them that hear thee."

The reason we concentrate on personal holiness and accurate teaching is twofold.

1. Perseverance

In what sense does personal holiness save us? In the sense of the perseverance of the saints. In John 8:31 Jesus says, "If ye continue in my word, then are ye my disciples indeed." Scripture repeatedly affirms that those who are genuinely saved will continue in the faith. Paul tells Timothy that if he continues in personal holiness and accurate teaching he will keep moving along the inevitable path of final and glorious salvation. He doesn't mean Timothy would become his own redeemer but that perseverance in godliness would guarantee that his faith is genuine.

John warns that those who appear to be believers and then depart were never truly saved (1 John 2:19). However, those who persevere inevitably give evidence of being truly saved.

2. Persuasion

If we persevere in godliness and truth, our lives will affect others; we'll bring them the message of salvation. We don't actually do the saving, but we are used by God as we preach the Word of God and live godly lives. That is the climax of 1 Timothy 4. All the qualifications of an excellent servant ultimately result in the salvation of souls. That is our purpose in life and the reason we remain in the world after we've been redeemed. If all God wanted was our worship, He could take us to heaven at the moment of our salvation. If the purpose of our salvation was just so that we could know Him, it would be better for us to go immediately to heaven, where we will know Him perfectly. If we were saved for perfect fellowship, our fellowship would be perfect in heaven. The only reason we've been left here is because we are the agents by which God brings the message of salvation to lost people. That's the sum of ministry. It's a high, holy, and glorious calling. I trust that by the power of God's Spirit we will experience its fullness in all our lives for His glory.

Focusing on the Facts

1. What is Paul's emphasis in 1 Timothy 4 (see p. 92)?
2. With what two things must a good servant of Christ be preoccupied (see pp. 93-94)?
3. An excellent minister is _____ _____ in his work (see p. 94).
4. What happens when a minister divides his efforts between the ministry and other interests (see p. 94)?
5. A servant of God is never _____ _____ (see p. 94).
6. True or false: It's important for a minister not to let his people see his faults (see p. 95).
7. True or false: We are unable to meet the Lord's standards for a servant of Christ on our own (see p. 96).
8. Are the standards in 1 Timothy 4 for pastors only? Explain your answer (see p. 96).
9. Paul commands Timothy to concentrate on _____ _____ and _____ _____ (see p. 97).
10. In what sense does personal holiness save us (1 Tim. 4:16; see p. 98)?
11. The Bible teaches that those who are genuinely saved will _____ _____ _____ _____ (see p. 98).
12. What is the ultimate purpose of all ministry (see p. 98)?

Pondering the Principles

1. In 2 Timothy 4:2 we learn that an excellent servant of Christ is to be ready to minister at all times, whether it is convenient or not. Do you find that there are times when you fail to minister to others because you don't want to be inconvenienced? Do you minister only when it is easy to do so? If so, spend some time this week meditating on 2 Corinthians 11:23-33, and consider some of the inconveniences the apostle Paul had to put up with in his ministry. Then ask God for His grace to enable you to minister in season and out of season.

2. Timothy was encouraged to allow others to see progress in his spiritual growth. He was to be open with people and not pre-

tend he had no flaws. How about you? Are you afraid to let those you minister to—your spouse, friends, or family—know the real you? Are you like the Pharisees, who gave the outward appearance of holiness but inside were full of uncleanness (Matt. 23:27)? If you struggle with that, realize that God knows who you are on the inside (cf. Ps. 139:1-4; 1 Sam. 16:7), yet accepts you. Armed with that confidence, dare to start being open and honest with other people.

Scripture Index

Topical Index

Amaziah, apostasy of. *See*
  Apostasy
Apostasy
  Amaziah's, 8, 20
  character of apostates
    hypocrisy, 16
    seared conscience, 16-17
  danger of, 14-15, 21-22
  dealing with, 10, 25-27
  definition of, 8-9
  inevitability of, 11-12
  source of, 9-10, 13-16
  subtlety of, 16
  teachings of apostates, 15-20
  timing of, 12-13
Asceticism, 17-20, 22
Athletics. *See* Exercise
Authority. *See* Preaching

Baxter, Richard, on work of the
  ministry, 51-52
Bible. *See* Scripture
Boldness. *See* Preaching, authority of
Brooks, Thomas, on importance
  of example, 61

Charismatic movement, cause
  of, 27
Christianity, raising low stan-
  dards of contemporary,
  58-72
Cochrane, Thomas, on wanting
  hardest mission field, 51
Commitment. *See* Service, com-
  mitment to
Communication. *See* Speech
Conduct, right. *See* Godliness
Conscience, seared, 16-17

Credibility
  in conduct, 62, 67-69
  in speech, 65

Discernment, importance of.
  See Apostasy, dealing
  with
Discipline, benefit of spiritual,
  32-37, 93-95

Exercise, limitations of physical,
  33-34, 37, 69

Fables, as opposite truth, 31-32
Fairy tales. *See* Fables
Faithfulness. *See* Service, commitment to
False teachers. *See* Apostasy
Flavel, John, on teaching relent-
  lessly, 82
Food
  being thankful for, 19-20
  blessing of, 18-20
  prayer and, 19-20
Fuller, Thomas, on power of example, 62

Gnosticism, its denial of physical pleasures, 18
God
  providence of, 49-50
  sense in which He is "Savior
    of all men" (1 Tim.
    4:10), 47-52
  sustaining power of. *See* pro-
    vidence of
Godliness
  importance of, 34-36, 61-72
  meaning of, 42-43

refutation of universal, 47-48
Sanders, J. Oswald
  on godly men, 32
  on mediocre ministers, 45
Satan and demons. *See* Apostasy, source of
Scripture
  accuracy of. *See* inerrancy of
  analogia scriptura. *See* consistency of
  application of, 80-81
  authority of, 53-56
  consistency of, 48
  devaluation of, 31-32
  explanation of. *See* exposition of
  exposition of, 78-82. *See also* Teaching
  having high view of, 53-56, 60-61
  inerrancy of, 55, 60-61
  interpretation of, 60, 80
  reading of, 77-80
  reliability of. *See* inerrancy of
  studying, 27-32, 59, 89-90. *See also* interpretation of
  teaching of. *See* exposition of
Seducing spirit. *See* Apostasy, source of
Self-denial. *See* Asceticism
Self-discipline. *See* Discipline
Self-indulgence. *See* Materialism
Service, Christian
  affirmation for. *See* confirmation for
  age for, 64-65
  attitude for, 24-25
  commitment to, 44-52, 55, 87-88, 90, 98-99. *See also* qualifications for
  confirmation for, 84-88
  disqualification from, 72
  excellence of, 24

  faithfulness in. *See* commitment to
  fun of, 69
  goal of, 97
  heart of, 97-98
  hope of, 46-47
  integrity in, 58-59
  materialism in. *See* Materialism
  motives for, 44-45
  positive nature of, 25
  price of, 44-46
  qualifications for
    avoiding false teaching, 31-32, 41-42
    being absorbed in one's work, 93-95
    being committed to hard work, 44-52
    being disciplined in godliness, 32-34, 42-43
    being virtuous, 41, 61-72
    fulfilling one's calling, 82-88
    having biblical ministry, 77-82
    progressively growing spiritually, 95-96
    teaching with authority, 52-54, 60-61
    studying Scripture diligently, 27-30
    warning people of error, 25-27
Speech, standards for, 65-66
Spiritual gifts
  affirmation of, 84-87
  definition of, 84-85
  sovereign bestowal of, 84-85

Teaching, 52-54, 60-61, 81-82. *See also* Preaching
Thankfulness, importance of, 18-20